Foucault, Marxism and History

Foucault, Marxism and History

Mode of Production
versus
Mode of Information

MARK POSTER

Polity Press

© Mark Poster, 1984

First published 1984 by
Polity Press, Cambridge, in association with Basil Blackwell, Oxford.

Editorial Office
Polity Press
PO Box 202, Cambridge, CB1 2BT, UK

Basil Blackwell Ltd
108, Cowley Road, Oxford, OX4 1JF, UK

Basil Blackwell Inc.
432 Park Avenue South, Suite 1505, New York, NY 10016, USA

British Library Cataloguing in Publication Data
Poster, Mark
Foucault, Marxism and History
1. Foucault, Michael
I. Title
194   B.2430.F.724

0–7456–0017–4
0–7456–0018–2 pb

Also included in the Library of Congress Cataloging in
Publication lists.

Typeset by
Styleset Limited, Warminster
Printed in Great Britain by
Billing and Sons, Ltd., Worcester

For my Mother, Claire

Alberich

Nibelung elves,
bow down to Alberich!
Now he is everywhere,
watching and spying.
Peace and rest
now have been banished.
Work for your master,
who watches unseen,
and when least you're aware
sees all of your actions.
You're his slaves,
now and forever.

Wagner, *Das Rheingold*

Contents

Preface and Acknowledgements

This book is intended as a set of essays examining the value of the recent works of Michel Foucault for social theory and social history. Foucault's works written since 1968 (*Discipline and Punish, The History of Sexuality* and numerous shorter pieces) contain some important advances in social theory and in the writing of social history. My purpose is to separate out those advances from other features of Foucault's thought which I find less beneficial. I am not attempting to give an assessment of Foucault's work as a whole but to focus on and analyse certain features of it.

To that end I situate Foucault's work in a double problematic: those of critical social theory and a new social formation that I call the mode of information. Although Foucault's politics may be ambiguous, his works are profitably situated in relation to critical theory. He provides, I will argue, models of analysis that contain theoretical elements which, properly interpreted, open up new directions for critical theory, directions that can lead it out of its current impasses. But these new directions only become apparent when certain important changes in the social formation of advanced industrial society are recognized. To that end I have coined the somewhat infelicitous phrase 'mode of information' to represent these changes and to contrast the current situation to Marx's concept of the mode of production.

Preface and Acknowledgements

The term 'mode of information' designates the new language experiences of the twentieth century brought about for the most part by advances in electronics and related technologies. This is not an essay on the mode of information and I have not attempted to elaborate the term into a full theory. Nonetheless I found it necessary to develop the term if only to illuminate the theoretical advances I find in Foucault's work and to contrast them with the traditions of critical theory based on the concept of the mode of production. In a future work I propose to offer a general theory of the mode of information.

The first two chapters attempt to situate Foucault's recent works in relation to Western Marxism and to the classical texts of Marx. The remaining chapters examine the relation of the theoretical developments in the early chapters to the historical texts of *Discipline and Punish* and *The History of Sexuality*. The utility of Foucault's writing for a new kind of social history is the point in question.

My research was facilitated by collegial and institutional assistance. A Fellowship from the National Endowment for the Humanities in 1981–2 was invaluable in furthering my work. I also received a Summer Faculty Fellowship from the School of Humanities of the University of California, Irvine, as well as several grants from the Focused Research Program in Critical Theory at UC Irvine. Friends and colleagues provided criticism and encouragement, especially Jonathan Wiener, David Carroll and Frank Lentricchia. Anthony Giddens and John Thompson, editors of Polity Press, were especially generous with their time and helpful with their comments.

Earlier versions of three chapters appeared in the following journals: Chapter 3 in *Social Research*, Vol. 49, Number 1; Chapters 2 and 5 in *Humanities in Society* Vol. 5, Numbers 3 and 4 and Vol. 2, Number 2 respectively. Their permission for later versions of these articles to appear in the present volume is gratefully acknowledged.

1

Foucault and Sartre

In the English-speaking world Foucault is often considered a post-structuralist. His ideas are examined in relation to those of Derrida and Lacan. Although there are good reasons for setting Foucault in the post-structuralist context, a compelling case can be made for an alternative strategy, one which depicts Foucault as a continuation of and departure from the Marxist tradition. In this book I shall consider only 'Western' Marxism. The juxtaposition of Foucault and Western Marxism is especially fruitful when one is considering Foucault's recent works, where the question of political commitment is in the forefront. *Discipline and Punish* and *The History of Sexuality* can be interpreted as Foucault's response to the events of May 1968 in France, exploring a new leftist political position in which the traditional critique of capitalism and advocacy of the working class were held in suspense. If Western Marxism emerged as the theoretical response to the impasses of classical Marxism confronting the events from World War I to the Cold War, Foucault's recent books may be seen as a theoretical response to the difficulties of Western Marxism in confronting the upheavals of the 1960s and the new social formation emerging thereafter.[1]

Western Marxism, a term coined by Merleau-Ponty in the postwar period, is defined most often as a response to the theoretical limitations of Leninism and the Social Democracy

of the Second International. Its origins go back to Georg
Lukács and Antonio Gramsci, but its chief manifestations
were the work of the Frankfurt School in Germany[2] and the
existential Marxists in France after World War II.[3] Broadly
speaking, the Western Marxists sought to redefine the place
of the subject in Marxist theory by confronting Marx's positions with recent intellectual developments such as psychoanalysis and existentialism. They also examined the epistemological difficulties in the Marxist dialectic by reassessing its
Hegelian roots[4] and restricting more than Marx had done the
metaphysical scope of dialectical thought.[5] Finally, they
shifted the attention of critical theory away from the means
and relations of production toward issues of everyday life
and culture. At every point a disturbing question pursued
them: were they still Marxists or simply disgruntled intellectuals? In general, their political allegiance to Marxist political
organizations was tenuous or non-existent. Theoretically,
their position as Marxists was at best ambiguous. It was rarely
clear if their work was supplementary to the classical Marxist
concept of the mode of production, or a thorough-going
revision of Marxist doctrine which adhered only to the
general spirit of the critique of political economy. These issues
were especially difficult to clarify in a political context where
the Western Marxists had no organic contact with class
struggles. The events of May 1968 changed everything,
because in these events a radical movement emerged outside
the parameters of the Marxist parties, providing a political
basis for a new critical theory. In this conjuncture the Western
Marxists could at last tabulate the balance sheet of their
relations to Marxism.

Foucault's intellectual trajectory kept him separate from
the Western Marxists until after May 1968. He complains that
his teachers never so much as uttered the words 'Frankfurt
School[6]', so that he was denied the opportunity of confronting a body of theory that he now thinks might have been of
great assistance to him then and continues to interest him.

The relation of Foucault to the French Western Marxists is however more complicated. Although a generation younger than Merleau-Ponty and Sartre, he was, like them, influenced by the Hegelian revival in the postwar years, since he studied with Jean Hyppolite, one of its chief representatives. He was also, like them, exposed to and attracted by German existentialism. His early work *Mental Illness and Psychology* (1954), was indebted to Ludwig Binzwanger, a psychologist who himself owed much to Martin Heidegger. Furthermore, Foucault's first major work, *Madness and Civilization* (1961), was animated by a critique of Western reason that was not entirely at odds with the anti-scientism of Sartre and Merleau-Ponty. Finally, like the existential Marxists, Foucault moved in and around the French Communist Party in the early postwar years. And yet, by the early 1960s, Foucault was much taken with structuralist currents of thought, tendencies which Sartre found so repellent.

Foucault's intellectual course thus ran somewhat parallel to that of the existential Marxists until the early 1960s. At that point he diverged radically from Sartre, considering his own position the antithesis of all philosophies of consciousness, including Sartrean existential Marxism. In this way the books of this period, *The Birth of the Clinic* (1963, though published in 1969), *The Order of Things* (1966) and *The Archeology of Knowledge* (written before May 1968), are ostensibly opposed to positions like Sartre's which rely on a theory of the subject. That much is certainly true. Yet even at this point of extreme opposition, I would maintain that it is possible to suggest certain similarities between Foucault and Sartre. Even though Parisian intellectuals understood Sartre as the antithesis of the new structuralist currents, both Sartre and the structuralists defined themselves in opposition to what has come to be called the Western metaphysical tradition. Sartre, after all, disputed the Cartesian concept of the rational subject as the epistemological and ontological ground of reality. While it is true, as the structuralists charged, that Sartre relied on what they saw as an idealist notion of the subject, it remains the case that the explicit intention of Sartre's thought, especially in the *Critique of Dialectical Reason*, was to undermine the metaphysical gounds of Cartesian reason, an intellectual direction akin to that of Foucault. It is also true that Foucault and others associated with structuralism denied the success of Sartre at this task. Yet during the 1970s, after the structuralist movement had passed its heyday, Foucault reconsidered the question of the subject, recognizing that, whatever the dangers it involved of a relapse into metaphysics, the question of the subject was impossible to avoid for critical theory. Without some theory of the subject (or subjects) it was not possible to account for resistance to authority.[7] What had to be avoided for Foucault was a notion of the subject as transcendental and unchanging over time, traces of which were still to be found in Sartre's later work.

In the 1960s Foucault was openly hostile to all forms of humanism and philosophies of consciousness, a hostility that was also directed against Western Marxism in general and Sartre in particular. When Foucault trumpeted the call 'man is dead', he would no doubt have included Sartre among the humanists he was defying. After 1968, however, Foucault's icy hostility to Sartre and Western Marxism melted away. He began to acknowledge the importance of their standpoint and to many observers Foucault, more than anyone else, had taken up Sartre's position in the Parisian intellectual and political world.

Until he bacame ill in the mid-1970s, Sartre had been the twentieth-century version of Voltaire, an intellectual of diverse talents who championed under the banner of justice the causes of the oppressed and without party or organization, did battle with the established order. Sartre, like Voltaire before him, enjoyed broad popularity and was therefore relatively immune from retribution by the authorities. It is clear that Foucault has never attained the celebrity status of

Sartre, but in the early seventies he began to champion the causes of several oppositional groups and to write political pieces for *Le Nouvel observateur.* He spoke on behalf of prison reform, and the rights of homosexuals; he supported the anti-psychiatry movement and the women's movement; he analyzed the importance of the revolution that overthrew the Shah in Iran.[8] During these years Foucault was perhaps the most eminent and widely-acknowledged intellectual who participated in leftist politics. Ironically, Foucault was at that time criticizing the role and function of the traditional intellectual.

Without understanding Foucault's new political status in the 1970s, his praise of Sartre in articles and interviews would be perplexing. Back in the 1960s a polite exchange of sorts took place between the two men in the pages of *La Quinzaine littéraire.* Sartre acknowledged the achievement of Foucault's *Les Mots et les choses,* but repeated a complaint he had registered against Lévi-Strauss: Foucault avoided the question of history, how one episteme is supplanted by another.[9] A few months earlier in the same journal, Foucault dismissed Sartre and Merleau-Ponty as 'courageous and generous' men of an earlier era, animated by a spirit that had passed from the intellectual scene.[10] Again in the same journal, in March 1968, only two months before the events of May, Foucault politely dismissed the 'enterprise of totalization' in philosophy from Hegel to Sartre, an enterprise no longer on the agenda.[11]

Foucault continued with a statement of characteristic modesty: 'I think the immense work and political action of Sartre defines an era . . . I would never accept a comparison – even for the sake of contrast – of the minor work of historical and methodological spade work that I do with a body of work like his.'[12] Yet the intellectual generation gap revealed in *La Quinzaine littéraire* was shortly to be bridged as both men worked together in the 1970s for the journal *Libération.*

After 1968 Foucault's attitude to Sartre and Western Marxism began to change. Sartre was not longer simply the philosophical enemy, as Foucault began to discover points of agreement and convergence of thought. In one interview Foucault praised the role that Sartre played in raising the intellectual and political consciousness of the French public: 'from the end of the war onwards . . . we have seen ideas of profoundly academic origins, or roots . . . addressed to a much broader public than that of the universities. Now, even though there is nobody of Sartre's stature to continue it, this phenomenon has become democratized. Only Sartre – or perhaps Sartre and Merleau-Ponty – could do it . . . The public's cultural level, on average, has really risen considerably.'[13]

Or here again Sartre is alluded to as a kind of leftist that Foucault identifies with: 'if the Left exists in France . . . I think an important factor has been the existence of a Left thought and a Left reflection . . . of political choices made on the Left since at least 1960, which have been made outside the parties. . . It is because, through the Algerian War for example, in a whole sector of intellectual life also . . . there was an extraordinarily lively Left thought.'[14] Foucault's reference here is clearly to Sartre, Francis Jeanson and *Les Temps modernes*, which was a center for opposition to the Algerian war at a time when the French Communist Party supported it. Foucault now sees himself as an heir to the existential Marxists who developed their leftist critique outside the CP. Speaking of his own debt to Nietzsche, Foucault is almost proud to find in Sartre a similar interest in Nietzsche. 'Did you know that Sartre's first text – written when he was a young student – was Nietzschean? 'The History of Truth,' a little paper first published in a *Lycée* review around 1925. He began\ with the same problem [as Foucault?] and it is very odd that his approach should have shifted from the history of truth to phenomenology, while for the next generation – ours – the reverse was true.'[15] Foucault imagines

Sartre and himself as children of Nietzsche, with the difference that Sartre strayed from the paternal heritage. Foucault identifies with Sartre as a brother and even regrets ('it is very odd that') their differences.

After May 1968 Foucault carried out a reorientation and clarification of ideas that substantially altered the direction of his work. I am not so much interested in the question of the unity or inconsistency of Foucault's thought, but rather in the theoretical direction of his work after 1968. I will argue that at this time Foucault came to grips with issues that were central to Western Marxism and that the positions he took, while in some cases resembling those of Western Marxists, generally went beyond their positions toward a new formulation of critical theory. In short, Foucault both came to terms with the problematic of Western Marxism and carried it to a new level.

AFTER MAY 1968

The events of May 1968 signified that an oppositional stance toward existing society was possible beyond the confines of contemporary Marxist orientations. During the month of May new groups participated in the protest movement, groups not traditionally associated with the proletariat. The events were sparked by students, continued by professional and technical workers, and supported by younger factory workers who were not the mainstays of the Marxist organizations. These groups relied on new methods of action, such as the tactic of provocation which served to reveal the weaknesses of the established order rather than to overthrow authority and take power. They developed new organizational forms, notably the Action Committee which was radically democratic and was oriented toward the enactment of new kinds of social relations rather than toward mobilizing the strength of the revolt. And finally they formulated a set of demands in their wall posters that constituted a post-Marxist critique of society. The ideology contained in the wall posters spoke not only against capitalism, but also against bureaucracy and all non-democratic forms of social organization. It contested not so much exploitation, but alienation. Its focus was not simply the factory, but all sectors of everyday life. It demanded not so much an equal share for all in the spoils of capitalism, but an active participation (*autogestion*) and creative role in all social action.[16]

For most leftist intellectuals, May 1968 constituted a break in the traditions of revolution. It became apparent that a new social formation was being born and that a new critical theory would be required to account for it and formulate an opposition to it. In addition, the opening cleared by May 1968 led to a profusion of new protest movements, not all of them specifically anticipated during the events of May themselves. The women's movement, the gay liberation movements, the movement for prison reform, the ecology and antinuclear movement, various regionalist movements and the anti-psychiatry movement all emerged in the early 1970s as responses to the events of May 1968. These new forms of protest created a new political mood, often characterized, in false imitation of the Chinese, as a cultural revolution. Traditional Marxism was woefully inadequate in accounting for the new aspirations, tending, if it dealt with them at all, to homogenize them into the labor movement. Foucault and others, like Deleuze, Guattari, Castoriadis, Lefort, Lyotard, Baudrillard, Morin and Lefebvre, took the situation more seriously and attempted to revise their thought in line with the new political exigency.

In Foucault's case, the themes of domination and power came to the fore. It has often been noted that, starting with his inaugural address at the Collège de France in 1970, Foucault began to stress the connection between reason and power. The *Discourse on Language* spoke of 'the institutional support' for 'the will to truth' and emphasized 'the manner in which knowledge is employed in society'.[17] More to the point, Foucault defined his future studies as genealogies of discourse in which discourse was to be understood as forms of power. 'The genealogical side of discourse . . . attempts to grasp it in its power of affirmation, by which I do not mean a power opposed to that of negation, but the power of constituting domains of objects.'[18] No longer would Foucault study only systems of exclusion, that which reason repressed; he would henceforth elucidate the mechanisms by which reason constituted and shaped forms of action. Power was no longer a negative, exclusionary function, but a positive formative one. In the 1970s Foucault's books on prisons and sexuality did just that.

Associated with the new concern with power and its new 'positive' definition was a tendency to associate reason with practice, a tendency that became more and more prominent after 1968. The structuralist concern with language and its autonomy that was prominent in *The Order of Things* (1966), gave way to an ill-defined but suggestive category of discourse/practice in which the reciprocal interplay of reason and action was presumed. Reason, manifested in discourse, was always already present in history. There was not innocent language whose internal mechanisms were a scientific paradigm that could serve as a model for social analysis, as we find in Lévi-Strauss's study of kinship. For Foucault, language organized as discourse was always associated with forms of discipline, disciplines that acted upon groups of humans and that in turn regulated the formation of discourse. This subtle yet ill-defined sense of the interplay of truth and power, theory and practice, became the central theme of Foucault's investigations. It characterizes his effort to go beyond structuralism and leads him into direct confrontation with the traditions of Western Marxism.

The purpose of presenting these indicators of change in Foucault's thought is not to prepare a brief for a detailed intellectual history. Instead, I have noted the new directions of his work after 1968 as a prelude to a systematic treatment of the relation of Foucault's work to that of Western Marxism. It should by now be clear that such a comparison is apposite and indeed crucial to current theoretical work. Foucault, finding support in Nietzsche, elaborated a new formulation of the thesis that reason is within history, a thesis that is central to Western Marxism. Whereas figures such as Sartre and Marcuse presented this thesis in a Hegel–Marx form, Foucault did so by resort to Nietzsche. The differences in their formulations are no less decisive than their similarities.

REASON IN HISTORY

The Western Marxists argued that reason was shaped by class-bound history. Both the positions of the theorist and those of any ideologies found in the world are regulated by class. For the later Sartre, to take one case, the situation of the thinker, his being-in-the-world, is in the last analysis a class situation, with the mode of production providing the final horizon of thought. The reason-in-history thesis effectively undercut the pretense of reason as arbiter of reality; it served as a kind of Kantian condition of possibility for thought that protected the thinker against the idealist tendency to ontologize reason. And yet this protection proved, in most cases, to be inadequate. For the tendency in the Hegel–Marx tradition, best exemplified perhaps in Lukács, was to subordinate the precautions of the reason-in-history thesis to the twists of the dialectic, arguing, through the back door, for an identical subject-object that all too frequently was another way of saying 'reason'. The historical dialectic moved through the class struggle; the class that represented the negation of the present was the privileged agent of history; the perspective of this class was therefore the true perspective, the perspective the theorist could adopt to grasp the totality. The theorist was then in a position to formulate the Truth. Such was the reasoning made possible by the Hegel—Marx thesis and such was the position taken by Lukács in *History and Class Consciousness*, a founding work of Western Marxism.

What saved the Frankfurt School, temporarily at least, from foundering on the same dialectical reef was their perception that the dialectic had deviated from its course of proletarian revolution. After Stalinism in Russia, the Welfare State in the West and especially after Hitlerism in Germany, Horkheimer, Adorno and, to a lesser extent, Marcuse became convinced that the working class was not the negation of capitalism and did not provide a privileged perspective on history. Reason was therefore without its condition of possibility. In response to this situation, members of the Frankfurt School took a different position. Marcuse, for instance, at times defined the traditional position (*Reason and Revolution*), at times sought through a special reading of Freud a new subjectivity in substitution for the working class (*Eros and Civilization*) and at times could not decide between the two (*One-Dimensional Man*). Adorno, perhaps more than any other figure in the Frankfurt School, sought to re-examine the difficulties of the Hegel—Marx thesis. In *Negative Dialectics* and *Against Epistemology*, he attempted to work through the reason-in-history thesis so that the reappearance of metaphysics would be prevented. Yet in both cases the Frankfurt School nurtured a certain nostalgia for the reason-in-history thesis that suggested a longing for a pre-Hegelian anchor. The privilege of reason was yielded reluctantly if at all. One finds in the writings of the Frankfurt School a clinging to the Enlightenment notion that freedom depends on the reason of the individual and the individual can exercise reason best in a condition of autonomy.

No one presents the case of the old notion of reason always lying hidden in the reason-in-history thesis better than Jürgen Habermas, perhaps the last representative of the Frankfurt School. Habermas has been more explicit in defense of the Enlightenment than the older generation of the Frankfurt

School. In his work on the history of communications one finds him postulating an ideal speech situation as the ground for a new, democratic public sphere in which the individual can exercize reason and attain the truth. For Habermas the ideal speech situation is always there in human communication, serving as a metaphysical support for reason.[19] Historical materialism, to him, suffers badly if it degrades reason to an epiphenomenon of the mode of production. More recently, Habermas has turned to systems theory, to theories of moral and psychological development to find a transcendental ground for the emergence of 'pure reason' in history. In this case, reason is once again inserted in history behind the back of classes and individuals, serving as a bulwark against tyranny and comfortably esconced as human nature.

Foucault ironically defends the reason-in-history thesis by giving it up. Foucault's Nietzschean skepticism about truth enables him to take a radical stance with respect to reason; there is not truth, only truths, and there is no epistemological ground upon which one can stand to ontologize reason, to grasp the totality and claim it all leads to this or that. But Foucault's radical skepticism does not lead to nihilism, because it enables him to search for the close connection between manifestations of reason and patterns of domination. The couplet discourse/practice presumes this connection as a condition for studying it, a hermeneutic circle that is unavoidable, though full of logical contradiction. Foucault can study the ways in which discourse is not innocent, but shaped by practice – without privileging any form of practice, such as class struggle. He can also study how discourse in turn shapes practice without privileging any form of discourse. Thus he writes a history of prisons in which Benthamite doctrine, responding to the Enlightenment reformer's horror at Old Regime punishment practices, in part leads to incarcerating institutions which develop their own system of power to manage inmate populations, and this in turn leads to new discourses (criminology) that study 'scientifically' and finally influence the administration of prisons. The inter-penetration of discourse and practice goes on interminably because they imply each other's existence from the beginning. In studying discourse it is not a question of perfect truth; in studying practice it is not a question of determining discourse. Both ontologizing tendencies are thus cut off from the start.

But Foucault's project would finally lead to nihilism unless a further dimension is given full recognition: the political dimension. For the couplet discourse/practice operates for the theorist as well as for the object studied. Foucault's discourse is also connected with politics. His own political motivation and situation shapes his discourse. He has recognized this explicitly:

> I would like to write the history of this prison, with all the political investments of the body that it gathers together in its closed architecture. Why? Simply because I am interested in the past? No, if one means by that writing a history of the past in terms of the present. Yes, if one means writing the history of the present.[20]

The important point is the following. Foucault's own situation is one in which discourses, like the ones he writes, are institutionalized as the human sciences and play a decisive role in the formation of practice (policy studies). In other words, Foucault has been able to develop the position that discourse and practice are intertwined in a world where domination takes the form of disciplines and discourse is organized into disciplines. In short, reason has become, in history, a form of power in a way that it perhaps was not before the eighteenth century. Foucault has come to terms with his situation, a world where the human sciences are organized and play a political role, by arguing for a position that looks at the human sciences only be de-ontologizing the concept of reason.

The Frankfurt School, in fact, began to recognize these same conditions. They were indebted to the work of Max

Weber in this regard. Whatever the merits of Weber's position, and there is a large body of literature arguing the case for and against, he made the strongest case for the association of reason and domination as the central trait of modern society. In opposition to Enlightenment assumptions, reason for Weber was not the handmaiden of freedom. In bureaucratic organizations reason was shaped into instrumental rationality and as such was compatible with authoritarian institutions (the state, the army, the corporation). The human being might be, as liberals claimed, a rational animal, but he was not necessarily a democratic one. The 'iron cage' of bureaucracy foretold a 'soulless' and 'spiritless' fate for human society.

Weber noted that modern society brought with it a new form of organization which he called bureaucracy. Unlike feudal social organizations, bureaucracy established an impersonality in social postions. Arranged hierarchically, these offices evoked a form of behavior that required a certain motivational attitude on the part of social agents, an attitude that appeared to conform to the liberal assumption about essential human rationality but when analysed further fell short of those hopes. Bureaucratic action, Weber contended, was indeed rational, but it was a special kind of rationality. In order to specify this rationality Weber created a set of modes of rationality, or 'ideal types', based on the means/ ends distinction. Action could be rational in its ends or in its means; bureaucratic rationality was the latter type. The ends of bureaucratic action were generated by the hierarchy, beyond the reach of most bureaucrats. In addition, these ends were defined by the organization itself: the goal of bureaucratic action was to continue the bureaucracy. More important to, and originating with, bureaucracy was a form of action defined by its means. Bureaucratic action was motivated by the efficiency of means; according to Weber it was oriented to accomplish goals with the least expenditure of effort and it required a continuous calculation of means.

Hence bureaucratic action was rational in that the means to attain goals were based upon calculations of efficiency. Bureaucratic action was instrumentally rational.[21] Georg Lukács, a student of Weber, expanded this analysis of means-rational action into a general critique of 'reification' in capitalist society.

Weber's analysis of instrumental reason, however bears only superficial resemblance to Foucault's position. For one thing, Foucault does not invent ideal types and then match them against historical experience. Forms of rationality for him might be infinite. In addition, the ideal type loads the historical dice: implicit in Weber's analysis is a Kantian prejudice in favor of ends-rationality, as might be recognized by recalling Kant's famous moral maxim that action must be motivated by universal ends.[22] Foucault prefers to show the limits of the present by juxtaposition with a different past, not with an ideal. In addition, Foucault does not analyse social agents and their motivations as Weber does. He is concerned with a level of objectivity that he calls discourse/practice, a category which avoids Weber's subject/object dichotomy and presupposes a non-duality between ideas and practice. Weber's analysis remains tied to a 'humanistic' assumption of the split between motive and action. Finally, Foucault's analysis aims at the discourses of the human sciences (one of which, sociology, was in some part founded by Weber), whereas Weber, however ambivalently, presupposed the separation of science and social action. Indeed, the main and perhaps only point of contact between Foucault and Weber rests in their effort to examine the implication of reason in domination.

The Western Marxists of the Frankfurt School addressed this problem at two points: in Horkheimer and Adorno's *Dialectic of Enlightenment* and in Habermas's critique of instrumental rationality, which, for my purposes, does not differ enough from Weber's position to justify separate treatment. *Dialectic of Enlightenment*, written after the Second

World War by refugee German Jews, bears the mark of the holocaust. No perspective on modern history could be adequate after Auschwitz if it portrays the past centuries as the march of reason. Given the brutality and bestiality of the twentieth century, Western civilization was hardly a drama of progress. Horkheimer and Adorno sought to undermine the liberal (and Marxist) faith in reason by drawing a connecting link between the inventiveness of Odysseus and the fabrications of the contemporary 'culture industry', placing particular emphasis on 'the achievements' of the eighteenth century. The Western form of reason, they admonished, presupposed a large measure of domination by positing the world (other human beings and nature) as an object to be controlled.[23] In the West a component of irrationality was inherent in the evolution of Enlightenment from the outset, an irrationality which emerged all too clearly in the politics and culture of the twentieth century.

While the analysis in the *Dialectic of Enlightenment* contains rich suggestions, especially the parts on the culture industry which Adorno in particular developed in ensuing essays, it is limited by its level of analysis. Too often Horkheimer and Adorno concern themselves only with the 'great thinkers' of the past, missing the mundane levels at which reason becomes discursive practice. Their highly philosophical analysis and critique of reason misses the chance to present a detailed view of the disciplines of truth. Nonetheless, their refusal to take reason at its word and their insistence on investigating its imbrication with domination leads directly to the problematic explored by Foucault.

FROM LABOR TO DAILY LIFE

In addition to problematizing reason, Western Marxists have in common with Foucault a shift of interest away from the mode of production toward the 'margins' of everyday life. In a recent interview Foucault identifies himself with the French Western Marxists and credits them in part for the electoral success of the Socialist Party in 1981:

> ... the Socialist Party was greeted so responsively in large part because it was reasonably open to ... new attitudes, new questions and new problems. It was open to questions concerning daily life, sexual life, couples, women's issues. It was sensitive to the problem of self-management, for example. All these are themes of Left thought — a Left thought which is not encrusted in the political parties and which is not traditional in its approach to Marxism.[24]

The themes of daily life provide the area for a revitalized critical theory. In France these themes were pioneered by Sartre and Merleau-Ponty in *Les Temps modernes*, Henri Lefebvre and Edgar Morin in *Arguments* and Cornelius Castoriadis and Claude Lefort in *Socialisme ou barbarie*.[25]

The major theoretical break in France came with Sartre's *Critique of Dialectical Reason* (1960), where the analysis of everyday life became the central concern of critical theory. In a period when the working class seemed to have abandoned its historical project as outlined by Marx, Sartre re-examined the question of revolution in terms of the conditions for a free form of subjectivity and the obstacles to it. He analysed the conditions in which a class disrupts its routines, focuses on its burden of subordination, envisages clearly a path to freedom and takes action to attain that end. To understand why these moments of revolutionary consciousness are so rare, Sartre investigated the modes of relationships and consciousness among subordinated groups in daily life. He hypothesized a form of interactive being termed 'the series'. In everyday life, the oppressed lie in a kind of group relationship in which each individual sees the other as a remote, hostile party. The individual posits him or herself with goals and purposes, such that others are merely obstacles. That we are in fact in groups Sartre argues with the example of reading the newspaper: many people do it and they do it at the same time, but they are in isolation even though they perform the same action at the same time. That we posit each other as obstacles Sartre argues by the example of the line of people waiting for a bus where each knows that the others might take a seat that could be his or hers. In these ways the population is atomized while remaining in groups and effectively deflected from attaining class consciousness.

The theme of atomization was richly explored by French Western Marxists during the 1960s. It was the major concern of Henri Lefebvre in books such as *Daily Life in the Modern World* (1968), and Guy Debord's *Society of the Spectacle* (1967). Books and articles were devoted to the topics of consumerism, urbanism, the family, sexuality, education and leisure, each attempting to understand how subordinated groups suffer domination and lose control over their communal existence. The theme of alienation developed in Marx's early writings was turned to repeatedly for conceptual guidance. But Marx restricted the scope of the concept of alienation to the worker in the factory; the Western Marxists employed it to clarify the conditions of many groups in daily life. The conclusion was inevitable: the workers suffer domination not only in the factory but in all sectors of life and the workers are not the only group to suffer domination. Women, children, the aged, students, minority groups, consumers, residents – atomization and alienation are widespread phenomena and these phenomena cannot be grasped by exclusive reference to the workplace, or by the categories that were developed to analyse the exploitation of labor. Marxism was doubly inadequate: its categories were not broad enough to reveal domination outside the workplace and the social formation had changed since the time of Marx, requiring a break with the classical themes of the critique of political economy even in the realm of work.

Once it was clear that forms of domination existed outside the workplace, the question arose of methods and theories adequate to the task of analysis. Lukács's theory of reification and Gramsci's concept of hegemony were studied. In more drastic departures from classical Marxism, existentialism and phenomenology, psychoanalysis, structuralism and semiology were all explored by Western Marxists. The general problem faced by Western Marxists was that classical Marxism was not easily transferable to realms of daily life beyond the workplace. They encountered a theoretical limitation of classical Marxism by which the specificity of domination outside the workplace was lost or slipped away through the closure brought about by the theory of the mode of production. Lukács, for example, had applied his theory of reification in the workplace to a general cultural critique of capitalism. But the mechanisms by which workers are treated as things in the capitalist economy are not the same as those by which bureaucracy positions the general population. And the literary expression of bureaucratized life, for instance in Kafka, did not conform to the stylistic tenets of realism which Lukács saw as the counterpart to the critique of reification.

In the case of Gramsci, the same problems obtained. His theory of hegemony was meant to account for the active role of ideology and politics (the superstructure) in the class struggle. Gramsci argued that under capitalism political domination is separate from economic exploitation. Unlike the feudal system, bourgeois civil society prescribes different locations for work and for force or coercion. The workers are not subject to the political will of the bourgeoisie in the way the peasants were to that of the nobility. Instead, capitalism asserts the hegemony or domination of the bourgeoisie through the mediations of politics and ideology. Although this line of thought can be very fruitful in drawing out the connections between politics and the economy, its theoretical strategy is to illuminate only those aspects of politics and ideology that are pertinent to the relations of production. Gender politics, for example, are in general not analyzable using the category of hegemony.

When the Western Marxists discussed aspects of daily life in terms of the category of alienation the same slippage back to the mode of production took place. One could show that consumers were alienated in the marketplace through advertising, that students were alienated in the classroom through the system of examinations, that women were alienated in the home through isolation and so forth. In each case, however, it was assumed that the source of alienation remained the workplace and that other forms of alienation were derivations from that source. Ultimately, the struggle over alienation in the workplace took priority and the specific forms of domination in everyday life would be taken care of almost automatically after the capitalist economy was overturned by the proletariat.

THEORETICAL SUPPLEMENTS TO MARX

Due to the theoretical closure inherent in Marxism, Western Marxists found it necessary to confront classical Marxism with the theoretical developments of the twentieth century. By supplementing Marxism with psychoanalysis or existentialism, the dialectic could perhaps be opened up. Sartre's efforts in this regard are particularly noteworthy. They reveal both the strengths and the limitations of the strategy of supplementation. In particular, Sartre's existential Marxism demonstrates the difficulty of joining two conceptual systems into a coherent whole and brings to light the dangerous underlying assumption in the effort, notably the category of totalization.

Sartre's Existentialism

Sartre, in the *Critique of Dialectical Reason*, noted the limits of Marxism in the analysis of everyday life and called for a strategy of supplementation.[26] If he were successful, the dialectic would become a totalizing theory that was not reductionist. Each sector of capitalist society would be given its due weight as a mediation in the overall dialectical scheme. The family, for instance, would be shown both as generating its own form of domination and as a sector in the totality. In order to account for the relative autonomy of each moment of the dialectic, it was necessary to elaborate, Sartre contended, a vast scheme of categories designed to prevent premature closures and reductionism. The key to this categorial apparatus was the concept of totalization. Sartre argued that an adequate critical theory must specify two moments of totalization: one at the beginning and one at the end of the analysis, one at the epistemological level and one at the ontological level. At the ontological level, it was presumed that at any given moment human history or society was a totalization in process, a structural whole built by human beings, a sum of the intentions of human agents, albeit a sum reflecting their alienation more than their direct aims. In addition, Sartre argued that the condition of this history was the ontological possibility that human beings could all will the same totalization (freedom), that they could act upon this intention to create a social order which would have that freedom as its purpose, and that they could thereby eliminate alienation (the effects of otherness) and produce a world in which they would become free subjects. It should be noted that Sartre was perhaps the last major thinker to propose this Hegelian possibility.

At the other end of the analysis, at the epistemological level, Sartre also argued for the necessity of totalization. He resorted to existential phenomenology to show that all perception requires totalizations, that an observer is always privileged in drawing together disparate acts in an historical field revealing a totalization, even though individual actors may not be cognizant of it. Like a commanding general in a battle, the knowing subject necessarily takes a view of the whole and sees the parts in relation to it. Each individual totalizes in the act of living and the knower does the same. Sartre maintained that human subjectivity was the activity of totalizing the field and this was the basis for totalizations by the theorist. Not that the theorist had automatic access to the totality, however. Instead, the theorist totalized because consciousness in each instance was free and therefore had the totality as a possible basis for commitment. Both as a perceiver who could draw together the disparate aspects of the field and as a conscious actor who could choose any number of possible courses of commitment, the human subject totalized. Accordingly, the responsibility and task of the theorist was to carry out totalization in the realm of knowledge. The theorist's totalization was not the perfect, certain, objective knowledge of God or Descartes, because the theorist was situated in a specific historical field and had a specific history. The theorist's totalization was profoundly his own, but it was also available to others who could chose to adopt it. In this way, dialectical reason was both subjective, limited by the situation of the theorist, and objective, a possible project for everyone.

With the category of totalization, deriving from existentialism, Sartre had reformulated Marxist epistemology. No longer could Marxism fall prey to scientism and present its case in objectivist terms. At the same time the totalizing dialectic preempted the reductionist step inherent in the theory of the mode of production. Each moment of the dialectic was preserved in its relative autonomy; forms of domination in the family, for instance, were not reducible to those of the workplace. Nonetheless, each mediation remained connected with the totalization, but in this case the totalization did not mean the destruction of capitalist relations of production. It meant instead the adoption by all subordinated classes of the goad of totalization itself, the creation by free subjects of a world without classes and domination. These subjects would recognize their freedom by their commitment to a free society and would make themselves into these free subjects through the practice of creating that society.

At one time in the 1960s Foucault regarded Sartre's scheme as an error of the grossest sort. Sartre had committed the most basic sin of founding knowledge on the basis of a philosophy of consciousness. All the illusions of the philosopher's position were reproduced by Sartre in embarrassing explicitness. In no sense, Foucault thought, could the philosopher—theorist create representations of his or her thought which could serve as the standard of knowledge. Sartre's rescue of Marxism by use of the lifeboat of existentialism was a failure that would certainly drown the endangered victim, critical theory. Exchanging the alleged certitudes of scientific Marxism for the preposterous subjectivities of existentialism was no basis for a renewed critical theory.

And yet there were elements of Sartre's position overlooked by Foucault, which went in the direction he wanted to carry critical theory. Foucault's work has been concerned with developing a form of knowledge which did not claim too much for reason, which was not subject to the Nietzschean critique of the philosopher's will to power. In some respects Sartre's dialectical reason conformed to these strictures. Sartre did not assert that dialectical reason led to objective knowledge; nor did he claim that the theorist developed certain knowledge of the totality. Sartre insisted that the theorist was situated, like everyone else, and that his or her knowledge was limited to the perspective, as Nietzsche would say, afforded by each individual's historical and social location. In the 1970s Foucault would write his books on prisons and sexuality, as we have seen, insisting on the rootedness of his project in the present.

Even with these possible points of concordance, there remain profound differences between Sartre and Foucault — most notably on the question of totalization. Foucault was so deeply concerned to limit the scope of the theorist's epistemological position that he refused to systematize his position or even to elaborate concepts to any great extent. He refused to explore at all the position from which he attained knowledge and at times went so far as to grant that he was a simple positivist in order to avoid the task of self-reflection. Sartre took a position at the other extreme: he found Marxism so in need of epistemological clarity that he based the entire edifice of critical theory on the act of knowledge. Because consciousness is free (or undefined), the individual totalizes his or her project and thus the entire effort of knowledge comes back to the individual's need to choose a course of action. The elaborate complexity of the totalization returns to the epistemological moment of the theorist's choice of himself or herself. Critical theory, however, compelling though it may be as an analysis of the historical moment, is no more than the personal voice of the theorist.

There is an element of intellectual honesty in Sartre's position that Foucault cannot afford to overlook. The position of the theorist is crucial to the knowledge he or she develops. If knowledge is presented as coming from no one and nowhere, regardless of the modest claims made for the validity of that knowledge, a certain duplicity is introduced into the text, a duplicity through which the text assumes an objective authority that Foucault for one would not want to claim. In the end, Sartre's insistence on the personal nature of his knowledge is more Nietzschean, more respectful of the danger that knowledge is a form of power by other means, than Foucault's withdrawal from the text in unreflexive modesty. Foucault's salutary warning not to treat his text as a police dossier becomes an excuse for hiding in an epistemological closet.

There are nevertheless good reasons for Foucault's elusiveness: in Sartre's hands the urge to self-reflection ends in the justification of the theorist. Starting from the simple need to define his consciousness, Sartre ends with an air-tight, over-blown system that commands allegiance from the oppressed of the world. The totalization of his situation leads to an imposing hulk of theorization that stands over the populace like a tyrant commanding action and commitment. What began for Sartre as an effort to reduce the scope of reason through a clarification of the Marxist dialectic, ends in a tremendous expansion of the power of the intellectual. Sartre's dialectical reason pre-empts the initiative from the movement of protest, compelling conformity to theory at the expense of free practice. The epistemological need of critical theory is to find a path between the reticence of Foucault and the forthrightness of Sartre, a path that will respect the limits of reason by acknowledging the situation of the theorist without hiding the reflexive presence of the author in the text.

Sartre and Foucault differ even more sharply on the question of the object of theory and again there are strong arguments on both sides. For Sartre, the social-historical field consists of a dialectical interplay of men and things. While Sartre pays some attention to the transformation of the world of things (the mode of production), his major concern is the world of human subjects (series, groups-in-fusion) and the introduction of otherness into subjectivity (alienation) by the mediation of things. The main issue for Sartre is subjectivity: how can human beings recognize and realize their freedom in the ongoing totalization of history? The emphasis in the *Critique of Dialectical Reason* is on the obstacles that subjects confront in the effort at self-recognition. In other words Sartre's focus is the conditions for resistance to domination, a focus that no doubt grew out of his experience with the Resistance during World War II and corresponds to the situation of an increasingly prosperous, advanced industrial society (France in the later 1950s), one that contained no substantial oppositional movement.

The object of theory for Foucault, while at first glance completely divergent from Sartre's, could be read as the opposite side of the coin of critical theory. Writing after the structuralist attack on the subject, Foucault, in the 1970s, favors objectivity as a field of investigation. He tries to make intelligible modes of domination or 'technologies of power' that escaped the attention of classical Marxism. Technologies of power, such as the Panopticon or disciplinary system, are composed of conglomerations of discourses and practices, minutely arranged for the control of the body and the mind. This level of intelligibility could not be approached by reference to the subject or forms of consciousness, but rather through a careful analysis of the field of objectivity. Foucault is in this respect firmly at odds with Sartre. Resistance and the modes of subjectivity associated with it are not a serious problem for Foucault, who simply asserts that opposition to domination is ever-present.[27] In the 1970s the impetus of May 1968 was succeeded by numerous forms of opposition, seemingly at every point of power in the social field, a marked difference from the situation in which Sartre wrote. Attention to the political conjuncture must not, however, sidestep the important theoretical issues that separate the two thinkers. Yet one could draw the conclusion that the respective concerns for resistance and analysis of domination are complementary, not necessarily contradictory.

The issue on which Sartre and Foucault do butt heads is not so much the field of investigation, but the status of the subject. Foucault remains suspicious of positions which rely on a centered subject as a source of intelligibility. Individual self-consciousness is ruled out as an object of knowledge, a requirement that is central to Foucault's projects of the 1970s. In *Discipline and Punish* he is able to locate his object, technologies of power, only by an investigation that puts aside the rationality or agency of the individual or group. He looks for mechanisms of discourse/practice that are out of phase with the self-consciousness of the individual. In *The History of Sexuality* he goes a step further, defining his object as discourse/practices through which the individual is constituted as the subject of truth. In this case the rational individual is seen not as a proposition to be defended (or refuted), but as the consequence of social-historical processes, not as the intentional goal and underlying basis of history but as its illusory result. In a social system such as ours, based on (1) the assumption of a rational human nature and (2) the dissemination of scientific disciplines which are implicated in power relations, the task of critical theory, for Foucault, is to show how the subject and the disciplines are constituted under the sign of the truth. In this context the rational subject could not be considered an origin or cause.

What is often forgotten is that Sartre began his career with a strategy which he maintained almost throughout. Sartre, who was considered the chief defender of the subject by the structuralists, defined himself in opposition to all philosophies of mind as early as 1939.[28] With his existentialist-phenomenological assumptions, Sartre opposed French academic idealism in which the rational subject was a metaphysical center. Instead, the phenomenologist posited consciousness as a relation, a lack which flowed out to things and the existentialist depicted human reality as dispersed in the world, ex-isting not centered in rationality. Sartre's major works, *Being and Nothingness* (1943) and *Critique of Dialectical Reason* (1960) continue and elaborate further this theme.

Sartre does, however, posit a center for the subject not in terms of rationality but in terms of meaning. Consciousness creates meanings, it produces meaning even as it is lost in the world with others. According to some theorists, such a view of the subject is essential for a post-structuralist critical theory. The problem with Sartre's position for a thinker like Foucault is that Sartre theorizes the subject who produces meaning in ontological rather than linguistic-social terms. Kristeva, for example, praises Husserl for 'the fact that he has drawn attention to this object-constituting subjectivity which produces positioned consciousness in the act of predication', but not for 'the metaphysical affirmation of "being" or "presence" as the origin of meaning'.[29] In Sartre's

case there is an effort to go beyond the ontological formulation of the meaning-producing subject of *Being and Nothingness* in the *Critique of Dialectical Reason*. Here Sartre
employs social and historical categories to indicate transformations in the modes of subjectivity, without completely
escaping the ontological level. In this sense, Sartre has moved
in a direction similar to that of Foucault and works with the
same problematic, without going as far as Foucault in sur-
passing the rational subject. For his part Foucault has still
not completely come to terms with the problem of subjectivity,
in that he has been unable to theorize the production of
meaning by subjects or account for resistance to domination.

Theories of Language

If phenomenological existentialism is one methodology
employed by Western Marxists to resolve the limitations of
classical Marxism, linguistics is another. In his book *Mytho-
logies*, Barthes demonstrates the power of structural linguistics
for an analysis of the languages of everyday life. He reveals
the ideological mechanisms at work in advertising, fashion
and numerous leisure activities. When daily life is viewed as a
field of linguistic meanings (semiology), a process is uncovered
whereby social institutions are naturalized, given the appearance of universality, and conflicts are hidden behind
masks of floating signifiers. Semiology, Barthes argues,
illuminates the mechanisms of domination in the processes
through which meaning is produced in daily life.

The work of elaborating semiology into a completed
critical theory was carried out by Jean Baudrillard. Continuing
the work of Barthes and also Lefebvre, Baudrillard develops
a theory of the historical transformation of modes of signification.[30] To demonstrate the linguistic mechanisms of
present-day consumer society is not enough. Unless the
morphology of linguistic forms is analyzed, it would appear
that certain language structures are themselves universal, a

position that runs counter to the tenets of historical materialism. In this spirit Baudrillard analyzes the historical origins
of the contemporary semiological mechanisms. In advanced
capitalism signifiers (words) are split off from signifieds
(meanings) and referents (things), just as other structuralist
linguists have shown. But this language pattern is a historical
phenomenon, going back to the Renaissance. Before that
time language was characterized by the use of symbols in
which all the linguistic elements were integrated, not split
asunder. Baudrillard relies especially on anthropological
evidence to support his contention.

The predominant linguistic form in advanced capitalism
is not the symbol but the signal. Since the linguistic elements
are fragmented, signifiers are able to 'float' as it were in the
space of social practice and be combined with signifieds and
referents at will. In fact, the process of production has been
transformed by these floating signifiers. Capitalists no longer
rely on 'use value', the imagined or real utility of a commodity,
to sell their products. Instead, in the process of advertising,
signifiers are attached to commodities seemingly at random.
Qualities that are desired by the population (sexiness, self-
confidence) are attributed to commodities irrespective of
their functionality or material utility. Thus shaving creams
promise sex appeal; deodorants guarantee self-confidence,
automobiles are a means to an active social life; soft drinks
are the key to community, love, popularity; and so forth.
The process has advanced to such a degree that the mode
of signification is central to the capitalist mode of production.

The mechanism of the signal, whereby signifiers are
attached to commodities, assures an immediate if unconscious response by the receiver of the message. The communications of advertising are mediated through electronic
conduits. The advertiser constitutes the subject by carefully
manipulating the structure of the message with the desired
goal of an immediate reception of the meaning, a reception

that precludes rationality. Signals short-circuit the process of critical thought; the consumer is not to weigh carefully the possible utility of a commodity (does the signifier in fact correspond to the referant?), but instantaneously assent to the message and hopefully purchase the product in an impulsive act of semiological consumption. Taken as a whole, signals constitute codes, Baudrillard maintains, into which the subject is inserted and from which there is no escape.

At first Baudrillard regarded his semiological critique as a supplement to standard Marxism: the capitalist mode of production, splitting use-values from exchange values, creates the conditions for the code. At a certain point it becomes necessary for the process of capital accumulation to create a consumer society. Once basic needs are met, capitalist growth requires the formation of new needs and turns to the signal for that end. The new needs of the working class are emotional and social, so capitalists offer love and community through the same products that had earlier promised faster means of transportation or better nutrition. The semiology of advertising reveals yet another stage in the dialectic of capitalism.

Almost as soon as he developed this position, Baudrillard became dissatisfied with it on the grounds of its reductionism. The mode of signification is not so closely tied to the mode of production. Very quickly he began to argue for the relative autonomy and then the complete autonomy of the mode of signification.[31] Marxism, he contends is committed to a productivist model of society, whereas the implications of critical semiology leads to an exchangist position. Meanings are created in the process of social interaction, as anthropologists like Mauss and Sahlins have shown, not through the process of production. Historical materialism is chained to a utilitarian/functionalist view of society which relegates pre-capitalist formations to subsistence positions. Only capitalism has solved the riddle of the surplus, reinvesting it to generate growth. But non-capitalist societies also generate surpluses, Baudrillard responds, with the difference that what they do with the surpluses (in potlatches or gift exchanges) is determined not by any utilitarian rationality but by the process of the exchange of meanings. The full analysis of the code, Baudrillard concludes, requires a theoretical divorce of the mode signification from the mode of production.

Baudrillard's work, manifesting the difficulty Western Marxists have in attempting to supplement classical Marxism, bears some resemblance to Foucault's position. They both seek to give full weight in a critical theory to language and they both seek to present linguistic experience in relation to historical-social action. Baudrillard's polemical attack on Foucault, *Oublier Foucault* (1977), ended all chance of dialogue between the two. Yet they are both concerned with the constitution of the subject in linguistic practice, a similarity that suggests possibilities for further investigation. Baudrillard himself did not pursue immediately his earlier positions, but went off on a different path, starting with *Symbolic Exchange and Death* (1976), a path that led him away from the concerns of critical theory.

Another Western Marxist who took a 'linguistic turn'[32] is Jürgen Habermas, the main figure of the Frankfurt School after the deaths of Horkheimer, Adorno and Marcuse. Habermas dissolves the Marxist concern with labor in an analytic division of labor, interaction, and language.[33] Once he abandoned the reductionism of the base/superstructure model, Habermas investigated the foundations of critical theory in terms of language. He argues that inherent in ordinary language is a truth criterion that could serve as a basis for democratic politics.[34] This truth criterion is located not at the grammatical or syntactical levels of language, but at what Habermas calls the pragmatic level, the level at which language is an act of communication. Unlike the semiologists Barthes and Baudrillard, Habermas is not interested in language as a code with an internal logic. Instead, he moves critical theory closer to the point where language and action intersect. 'Communicative interaction' is the field that he investigates. While this strategy is certainly suggestive for critical theory, Habermas does not take full advantage of it. The fruitful line of investigation would be to look at changes in speech situations, especially those brought about by the electronic technologies of the recent past. Instead, as we have seen, Habermas is interested only in an 'ideal-speech situation' which serves as a foundation for the autonomous rational individual.

Even though Habermas and Foucault are often seen as the main figures of critical theory and debates have been arranged between them in hopes of furthering theoretical work, there is not much agreement in their positions. For Habermas is wedded to the Enlightenment value of individual autonomy through reason, while Foucault questions the relation of reason and democracy. Habermas, furthermore, resorts to transcendental grounds for theory, such as the ideal speech situation, while Foucault is more rigorously historical, preferring to trace the emergence of differing patterns of discourse/practice without privileging any. Habermas is more systematic theoretically and utopian politically, while Foucault is suspicious of systems and reticent about the elimination of domination in the future. All in all there is not much room for agreement between them and Habermas' position increasingly appears as a Kantian step backwards for critical theory.

Psychoanalysis

The third important methodology associated with the Western Marxist effort at theoretical renewal is psychoanalysis. Freud's ideas have been very popular with critical theorists since the early attempt by Wilheim Reich to synthesize historical materialism and psychoanalysis. Although Reich had little association with the Frankfurt School, Horkheimer was interested in Freud's thought and organized a project, with the important participation of Erich Fromm, to study the relation between authority and the family along psycho-analytic lines. Since the publication of *Studies on Authority and the Family* in 1935, Frankfurt School theorists returned again and again to the problem of reconciling Marx and Freud. In this vein there are Adorno's essay on social psychology, Marcuse's *Eros and Civilization* (1955) and *Five Lectures. Psychoanalysis, Politics and Utopia* (1970), and Habermas's *Knowledge and Human Interests* (1971).

Aside from Habermas, who is concerned with the epistemological value of the therapeutic experience, the themes treated by the Frankfurt School are similar, though there are important differences in emphasis. In general they applaud psychoanalysis for providing a mediation between the understanding of the individual and society. Freudian categories lead, they contend, to an appreciation of the significance of the superstructure: consciousness, ideology and sexuality. Psychoanalysis explains, as Marxism cannot, regressions in history – best exemplified by German fascism, but also by the infantile longings elicited by the culture industry.[35] The central theme in the Frankfurt School's use of psychoanalysis is, however, the notion of sexual repression. Marcuse and others expand the Marxist critique of capitalist political economy with a Freudian critique of bourgeois libidinal economy. In *Eros and Civilization*, Marcuse translates Freudian categories into a Marxist lexicon. Hence the reality principle becomes the performance principle and the parallel with Marx's surplus value is Freudian surplus repression. By means such as these, the Frankfurt School adds the critical value of psychoanalysis to historical materialism without presenting an internal critique of either position. Although many important essays resulted from this intellectual direction, it does not evoke a re-evaluation of either position, or lead to a redefinition of the requirements of a critical theory of society.

In Foucault's writing psychoanalysis appears in an entirely different register. Instead of using Freud's theory in his historical essay on sexuality, for Foucault, psychoanalysis is part of that history. He is critical in particular of the hypothesis of sexual repression that is associated with the Frankfurt School and with Reich. Given his theory of discourse Foucault maintains that bourgeois culture does not repress sexuality, but through the spread of discourses on sex, including psychoanalysis, forms of sexual practice are created. The subject is formed as one for whom sexuality is his or her truth, the deep secret of the self that is ultimately its center. In addition, psychoanalysis plays a role in Foucault's history of sexuality as a mechanism of discourse/practice not totally unlike the confessional, a power relation where the client/ subject is constituted and reconstituted in the discourse of the therapeutic situation. Foucault denies any animus toward Freudian theory, yet his *History of Sexuality* promises to provide a devastating critique of this human science that claims to be one of liberation from repression, but practices and enacts a mode of domination.

In France the appreciation of Freud had to wait until the 1960s[36] when interest was stimulated by the importance of Wilhelm's Reich's ideas by thinkers such as Jean-François Lyotard[37] and by the development of a peculiar form of psychoanalysis mixed with Hegelian phenomenology and linguistic structuralism that is associated with the work of Jacques Lacan. For our purposes, Lacan's importance rests with his influence on Althusser, Baudrillard and Deleuze/ Guattari. In Lacan's complex and often opaque formulations, the subject is constituted in the unconscious through a process mediated by language, which fixes the subject in decentered misrecognition of itself. In *Anti-Oedipus: Capitalism and Schizophrenia* (1972), Deleuze/Guattari expand and reverse the Lacanian position to present an elaborate critique of advanced capitalism. Like Foucault (and perhaps this was the basis for their association in the early 1970s), Deleuze positions psychoanalysis within the field of his critique, interpreting it as a form of libidinal 'territoriali-

zation' or 'coding'. Far from providing a means of comprehending psychic formation, the Oedipus complex is a parental
vehicle for at the same time eliciting and suppressing the
sexuality of the child. In capitalist society the natural flux of
the libido is coded in the family where in earlier social formations it is territorialized directly by politics. The aim of
Deleuze/Guattari is to 'de-territorialize' the libido, liberating
its schizophrenic flux.

Even though Foucault cannot be identified with such
Reichian politics of sexual liberation, there are moments
when his argument comes close to that of Deleuze/Guattari.
In *The History of Sexuality Vol. 1*, after a long discussion of
the way sexual discourses are forms of domination that draw
the subject into particular modes of sexuality, Foucault
raises the question of liberation from sexual domination.

> We must not think that by saying yes to sex, one says no to
> power; on the contrary, one tracks along the course laid out by
> the general deployment of sexuality. It is the agency of sex that
> we must break away from, if we aim — through a tactical reversal
> of the various mechanisms of sexuality — to counter the grips of
> power with the claims of bodies, pleasures, and knowledges, in
> their multiplicity and their possibility of resistance. The rallying
> point for the counterattack against the deployment of sexuality
> ought not to be sex-desire, but bodies and pleasures.[38]

This passage, so difficult to interpret, contains a rare example of utopian political thinking in Foucault's texts.
He writes not simply of resistance to power, which is unusual for him, but lalso of overturning domination (in the
area of sex) and establishing a new liberating regime (of
sex), a possible political statement perhaps without parallel
in his major writings.

It is clear that when he speaks of 'the deployment of
sexuality' he signifies the contemporary forms of discourse/
practice which constitute the 'sexuality' of the subject. In
other words, our culture generates specific modes of sex

which Foucault labels 'sexuality'. Against the Frankfurt School's thesis of repression and in common with Deleuze/ Guattari, Foucault includes the so-called 'sexual liberation movement' as part of the dominant form of sexuality.[39] Hence to affirm one's sexuality and reverse Victorian prudery is not an act of liberation but a move within the dominant discourse, an act that does not liberate the individual from opression, but rather fortifies him or her within it. The point of interpretive difficulty and textual surprise occurs when Foucault offers an alternative practice that would, he thinks, be liberative. We must remember that Foucault argues effectively against making such statements by claiming that that is not the role of the intellectual: the oppressed subjects must speak for themselves. Nevertheless, in this context, Foucault shifts voices and writes as a political subject, not merely as an analyst of politics.

Foucault trumpets the 'counterattack' against the dominant form of sexuality with the sounds 'bodies and pleasures'. Normally Foucault speaks of bodies as always within discourse/practice, never as innocent or natural, never outside social forms. Yet in this passage he seems to rely on a notion of the body which prefigures social domination. Like Deleuze/ Guattari's concept of the free flux of libido, Foucault here falls back upon the body as a point of resistance to sexual authority. If this is so, the prevalent understanding of Foucault as a pessimist who sees no escape from domination must be revised. Instead, he must be viewed as one who posits the possibility of resistance to domination and the elimination of domination, for that is what is presupposed in his call to arms of 'bodies and pleasures'. And yet this revolutionary statement, this 'tactical reversal', sits motionless in the text smugly looking out at the reader with an expressionless, enigmatic stare. Foucault refuses to develop the statement at all. The reader never finds out what is the nature of 'bodies and pleasures' that have escaped the 'deployment of sexuality', never learns the basis of the resistance (underlying innocence, natural powers, lididinal flux, unconscious drives, and so forth).

The passage in question reveals a central tension in Foucault's position, one that provides an important comparison with the Western Marxists. Like them, Foucault writes critical theory which illuminates modes of domination. Like them, Foucault is dissatisfied with both classical Marxism and the official Marxisms of 'actually existing socialist societies'. Like them, Foucault argues for the possibility of change, change which would eliminate domination. Like them, Foucault sets the epistemological limits of his text in the situation of the writer. Unlike the Western Marxists, however, Foucault refuses to investigate the sources of resistance. He rejects in turn Sartre's notion of free totalization; Marcuse's notion of erotic sensibility; Habermas's notion of the ideal-speech situation; and the general Western Marxist commitment to a concept of dialectics. Though he is right to be skeptical of these grounds of revolution, he nonetheless faces the problem that he cannot avoid completely some reliance on a notion of a resisting subject. As a result he slides into a celebration of 'bodies and pleasures' without having the theoretical justification for doing so.

Althusser

A comparison of Foucault with Althusser, another theorist in the camp of Western Marxism, reveals with particular clarity the extent to which Foucault has continued and broken away from the problematic of Western Marxism. Althusser, unlike Sartre, comes to terms with structuralism and language theory, arguing that Marx had anticipated these trends. In works after 1845, *The German Ideology* and *Capital*, Marx and Engels, according to Althusser, shed their Hegelian skins and established the science of historical materialism by theorizing the object (the mode of production) without resort to the subject,[40] an achievement that appears

to parallel that of Foucault. Althusser maintains a commitment to science in a way that the Nietzschean Foucault does
not; but in eliminating the metaphysical support of the
rational subject their work bears some similarity.

After dismissing the problem of the subject in his work of
the 1960s, Althusser found himself returning to that topic
after May 1968. In his essay of 1970, 'Ideology and Ideological
State Apparatuses', Althusser approaches the concept of the
subject through Lacan's linguistic Freudianism. First Althusser,
like other Western Marxists, rejects the classical Marxist
formulations of the problem of ideology. The base/super-
structure distinction, with its allowance only for the relative
autonomy of the superstructure, is replaced by the problematic of reproduction. The role of ideological formations
emerges clearly when the question of the reproduction of
the relations of production is posed. One can then focus on
the mechanisms through which hegemony is maintained.
Althusser reasons that ideology promotes reproduction by
establishing the subject as a subject in an imaginary relation
to society. Ideology provides the subject with the illusion
that it is a center of meaning, so that the subject lives its
relation to society in a way that reproduces the existing
class struggle. But ideology is not understood as pure ideas;
it makes its appearance only in practice and is institutionalized
or materialized in what Althusser calls 'Ideological State Apparatuses' (school, family, politics, law, trade unions and
communcations media).[41]

Althusser's formulation of the problem of the subject as
constructed through mechanisms of practice that invoke
ideology reveals a certain similarity with Foucault's theory
of discourse/practice. Foucault, like Althusser, grants no
truth value to discursive systems, regarding them as mechanisms of power that constitute subjects. Both thinkers are also
alike in refusing to divide ideas and action into separate
realms. And both are concerned with unmasking systems of
domination. But there the parallels end. Foucault gives more

weight to discourse, since for Althusser ideology remains a functional category (reproducing class relations) without much inner complexity or interest. So long as ideology satisfies the criteria of positing a centered subject, Althusser wants little more to do with it. Foucault investigates more concretely the specific forms of subjectivity constituted by discourse. For in the end, Althusser is concerned only with the effects of ideology on the working class, whereas Foucault investigates diverse social groupings, i.e. prisoners, homosexuals, the insane and medical patients.

Underlying these differences between Foucault and Althusser is a more fundamental one having to do with their relative commitments to Marxism. As a Marxist, Althusser theorizes the totality through the category of the mode of production. Foucault, rejecting the category of totality in general and the Marxist version of it in particular, refuses to limit himself to an analysis of the working class. The category discourse/practice is thus not inserted into a totalized theory but floats like a hawk over the social historical process, ready to swoop down upon any topic that seems appropriate. The theoretical choice offered by these two theorists is dramatic and urgent. In my view Foucault's position in the present context is more valuable as an interpretive strategy and ultimately, although this may strike a discordant note, more Marxist. If by Marxism one means not the specific theory of the mode of production or the critique of political economy, and not even the supposed dialectical method, but instead a critical view of domination which as historical materialism takes all social practices as transitory and all intellectual formations as indissociably connected with power and social relations – then Foucault's position opens up critical theory more than Althusser's both to the changing social formation and to the social locations where contestation actually occurs. In a world where social processes increasingly depend on information processing and where protest is diffused in multiple non-centered sites, a

totalization through the determination in the last instance
of the economy, such as Althusser's, is more mystifying
than heuristic.

The conclusion is inescapable that Foucault is continuing
the work of the Western Marxists by other means. Rejecting
almost the entire intellectual edifice of critical theory,
Foucault nevertheless remains within its problematic. The
crucial theoretical question that remains is, To what extent
does Foucault's rejection of so much of the Western Marxist
tradition of critical theory lead to a gradual dissipation of
that tradition or to a renewal of critical theory along new
lines?

Before engaging this question directly I want to explore
the fault lines of classical Marxist theory, to look for those
places in the Marxist position that in the present context are
obstacles to critical theory. In particular I will analyze
systematically the Marxist concept of labor in the context
of an advanced industrial society increasingly dominated by
what I call the mode of information. In establishing the
limitations of the Marxist position on this question, I will
point to the places in Foucault's work that provide avenues
of advance.

NOTES

1. Perry Anderson, *Considerations on Western Marxism* (London:
   New Left Books, 1976) and for a different view, see Russell Jacoby,
   Dialectic of Defeat: Contours of Western Marxism (New York:
   Cambridge University Press, 1981).
2. Martin Jay, *The Dialectical Imagination: A History of the Frank-
   furt School and the Institute of Social Research, 1923–1950*
   (Boston: Little, Brown and Co., 1973) and David Held, *Intro-
   duction to Critical Theory: Horkheimer to Habermas* (Berkeley:
   University of California Press, 1980).
3. Mark Poster, *Existential Marxism in Postwar France: Sartre to
   Althusser* (Princeton: Princeton University Press, 1976).

Foucault and Sartre   41

4. Herbert Marcuse, *Reason and Revolution: Hegel and the Rise of Social Theory* (New York: Oxford University Press, 1941).
5. Theodor Adorno, *Negative Dialectics*, trans. E. B. Ashton (New York: Seabury Press, 1973, original edition 1966) and Jean-Paul Sartre, *Critique de la raison dialectique* (Paris: Gallimard, 1960).
6. Georges Raulet, 'Interview with Michel Foucault', *Telos*, No. 55 (Spring, 1983), p. 200 and Michel Foucault, 'Afterword: The Subject and Power', in Hubert Dreyfus and Paul Rabinow, *Michel Foucault, Beyond Structuralism and Hermeneutics* (Chicago: Univeristy of Chicago Press, 1983) for a statement by Foucault on his political position prior to his death.
7. Michel Foucault, *Power/Knowledge: Selected Interviews and Other Writings, 1972–1977*, ed. Colin Gordon (New York: Pantheon, 1980), pp. 142, 117.
8. For a sample of these writings see 'Manières de justice', *Le Nouvel Observateur*, No. 743 (February 5, 1979); 'Un plaisir si simple', *Le Gai Pied*, No. 1 (April 1979); 'Lettre ouverte à Mehdi Bazarga', *Le Nouvel Observateur*, No. 752 (April 9, 1979); and 'Inutile de se soulever?', *Le Monde*, May 11–12, 1979).
9. *La Quinzaine littéraire*, No. 14 (October, 1966), p. 4.
10. *La Quinzaine littéraire*, No. 5 (May 16, 1966), p. 14.
11. *La Quinzaine littéraire*, No. 46 (March 1, 1968), p. 20.
12. Ibid., p. 21.
13. Georges Raulet, 'Interview with Michel Foucault', *Telos*, No. 55 (Spring, 1983), p. 210.
14. Ibid., p. 209.
15. Ibid., p. 204.
16. For a more complete analysis of May 1968, see Poster, *Existential Marxism in Postwar France*, Chapter 9 and also Arthur Hirsh, *The French New Left: An Intellectual History from Sartre to Gorz* (Boston: South End Press, 1981). For a selection of documents from May 1968, see Alain Schnapp and Pierre Vidal-Naquet, *The French Student Uprising: An Analytical Record*, trans. Maria Jolas (Boston: Beacon Press, 1971, original edition 1969).
17. *The Archeology of Knowledge and the Discourse on Language*, trans. M. Sheridan Smith (New York: Pantheon, 1972), p. 219.
18. Ibid., p. 234.
19. *Communication and the Evolution of Society*, trans. Thomas McCarthy (Boston: Beacon Press, 1979, original edition 1976) and

The Theory of Communicative Action, Vol. 1. Reason and the Rationalization of Society, trans. Thomas McCarthy (Boston: Beacon Press, 1984).

20. *Discipline and Punish*, trans. Alan Sheridan (New York: Pantheon, 1977, original edition 1975), p. 31.
21. Selections of Weber's classic formulations may be found in H. H. Gerth and C. Wright Mills (eds), *From Max Weber: Essays in Sociology*, trans. the editors (New York: Oxford University Press, 1958). Informative discussions of Weber's position are found in Wolfgang Mommsen, *The Age of Bureaucracy: Perspective on the Political Sociology of Max Weber* (New York: Harper and Row, 1974); Anthony Giddens, *Capitalism and Modern Social Theory* (New York: Cambridge University Press, 1971); and Jeffrey Aiexander, *Theoretical Logic in Sociology, Vol. 3. The Classical Attempt at Theoretical Synthesis: Max Weber* (Berkeley: University of California Press, 1983).
22. *Fundamental Principles of the Metaphysic of Morals*, trans. Marvin Fox, (New York: Bobbs-Merrill, 1949, original edition 1785).
23. Max Horkheimer and Theodor Adorno, *Dialectic of Enlightenment*, trans. John Cumming (New York: Seabury, 1972, original edition 1944), p. 6 and *passim*.
24. *Telos*, No. 55 (Spring, 1983), p. 209.
25. These developments are traced in Mark Poster, *Existential Marxism in Postwar France*.
26. This argument is made in *Search for a Method*, trans. Hazel Barnes (New York: Knopf, 1963) which appeared as the introduction to the *Critique* although it was first published separately.
27. In an interview entitled 'Powers and Strategies', he affirmed, ' ... there are no relations of power without resistances ... ' Trans. in Foucault, *Power/Knowledge* ... , p. 142.
28. 'Une Idée fondamentale de la phénoménologie de Husserl: l'intentionnalité', *Situations I*, (Paris: Gallimard, 1975, original edition 1947), pp. 38–42.
29. Cited in Rosalind Coward and John Ellis, *Language and Materialism: Developments in Semiology and the Theory of the Subject* (London: Routledge and Kegan Paul, 1977), p. 132.
30. *For a Critique of the Political Economy of the Sign*, trans. Charles Levin (St. Louis: Telos Press, 1981, original edition 1972).

31. *The Mirror of Production*, trans. Mark Poster (St. Louis: Telos Press, 1975, original edition 1973).

32. Martin Jay, 'Should Intellectual History Take a Linguistic Turn?: Reflections on the Habermas-Gadamer Debate', in D. LaCapra and S. Kaplan (eds), *Modern European Intellectual History* (Ithaca: Cornell University Press, 1982), pp. 86–110.

33. 'Technology and Science as "Ideology"', in *Toward a Rational Society*, trans. Jeremy Shapiro (Boston: Beacon Press, 1970, original edition 1968).

34. *Communications and the Evolution of Society*.

35. See, for example, Theodor Adorno, 'On the Fetish Character in Music and the Regression of Listening', in Andrew Arato and Eike Gebhardt (eds), *The Essential Frankfurt School Reader* (New York: Urizen, 1978), pp. 270–299.

36. Sherry Turkle, *Psychoanalytic Politics: Freud's French Revolution* (New York: Basic Books, 1978), p. 157.

37. For example, *Dérive à partir de Marx et Freud* (Paris: 10/18, 1973).

38. Michel Foucault, *The History of Sexuality, Volume 1*, trans. Robert Hurley (New York: Pantheon, 1978), p. 157.

39. Marcuse, of course, reversed his earlier position in *Eros and Civilization*, coming to see the sexual revolution as a product of 'repressive desublimation' brought about through the channeling of sexual drives in late capitalist society. *One-Dimensional Man* (Boston: Beacon Press, 1964).

40. *Reading Capital*, trans. Ben Brewster (London: New Left Books, 1970, original edition 1968).

41. 'Ideology and Ideological State Apparatuses', in *Lenin and Philosophy and Other Essays*, trans. Ben Brewster (London: New Left Books, 1971), p. 137.

2

Mode of Production, Mode of Information

If Foucault's recent works derive from and surpass the Western Marxist tradition, they also present a formidable challenge to the classical Marxist theory of history. Before assessing the value of Foucault's critical theory for the writing of social history, I want to examine and assess the position of Marx. From the perspective of the critical theory of society, a questioning of the value of Marxism is long overdue. Marxism itself may now be an obstacle to social criticism. What is needed is a relentless, systematic critique of Marxism, one that roots out those features that were problematic from the beginning, those that have become obsolete, and those that have proven themselves inadequate for the task, while preserving those that retain their critical powers.

The historical changes of the late nineteenth and twentieth centuries call into question many features of the Marxist position. Indeed, Marxism is haunted by the specter of history. Marxism has changed history, but so too has history changed Marxism. Emerging in the midst of industrial capitalism in the nineteenth century and proclaiming itself the gravedigger of that society, Marxism today fails to inspire the revolutionary will of the proletariat in the centers of advanced capitalism. It has proved itself instead the great hope of the colonized urban and rural masses in largely pre-industrial social formations. Marxist theory foretells the advent of communism in the developed capitalist social formations, those places where the organic composition of capital is weighted towards machines not labor, where the immiseration of the proletariat exacerbates social contradictions, where the rate of profit has long been declining, where all society has come under the rule of the commodity. Yet precisely in these places, where liberalism has long been relegated to the status of an historical curiosity, Marxism too appears to be a relic out of the past.

Confronted with these changes Marxist theorists often turn a deaf ear. Marxism is not only a movement; it is also a theory. Marxism raises history to an epistemological principle, but history in turn calls into question the truth-value of some Marxist categories. More than anyone before him Marx opened philosophy to the world, bonded theory to practice, intertwined reason and history. Marx posited the theoretical necessity of taking the situation into account, establishing the context as the pretext of thought. Science could develop, he contended, only by adopting the point of view of the pro-letariat. For Marx this theoretical act was not moral but epistemological. In order to avoid the pitfalls of ideology, that is, the intentional or unintentional justification of the world as it is, Marx elevated history to the status of a con-dition of knowledge. Only by comprehending the world as a transitory social formation, therefore as an historically limited phenomenon, could philosphy achieve scientific truth. The historical-social world becomes the internal limit of reason, the nontranscendental foundation of the categories of thought. And yet today Marxists are seemingly unable to respond to changes in the world. What Sartre long ago said of Stalin applies now more generally: Marxists are idealists who continuously restate Marx's categories, who confront the world with the theory of the mode of production, in-sulating reason from history and saluting the hegemony of Marx's thoughts over a world that has long since belied them. Even beyond the reach of governments that proclaim them-selves socialist, Marxists act like the bishop in Brecht's *Galileo*, refusing to look through the telescope for fear of discovering that reality refutes cherished illusions.

In the critique of Marxism, what must be avoided are the traditional stances in opposition to Marx, and these are many. There are classical anarchism and Trotskyism which find a moral flaw in some aspect of Marxism, the former rejecting it completely, the latter seeking to reconstitute it whole outside the evil of Stalin. There is the Frankfurt School stance of benign neglect of Marx's texts. Here the basic anti-capitalist impulse is kept, but the object of critique shifts to the superstructure. With the possible exception of Adorno, the Frankfurt School retains the fundamental premises of historical materialism, never questioning them directly but instead refining and elevating the level of critique. There are also the existential Marxists, among whom I counted myself at one time, who preserve the totalizing power of Marx while expanding the scope of the theory through the concept of mediations. Here again certain limitations of the theory are acknowledged, without, however, a complete commitment to their critique. There are, finally, a host of basically political postures against Marx which focus on the practice of specific socialist regimes and find them wanting in some regard. In this case the critique is limited to an attack on the leadership of the proletarian movement, or to a specific version of it such as the Social Democrats, the Bolsheviks, the Maoists. This strategy too leaves untouched the theoretical premises of Marx and assumes that, though mistakes have been made elsewhere, one can do it right when the time comes. Of course the time never comes as Chronos continues uninterruptedly to mow the wheat of capitalist history.

The first assumption in Marx's texts that needs to be questioned is the notion of human beings acting upon nature. Marx constitutes the social field as one in which human beings act upon natural materials to produce useful objects. This is, of course, the activity of labor from which Marx derives the entire complex of ideas known as the mode of production, as well as those ideas associated with the critique of political economy. In *The German Ideology* the figure of laboring man and woman is posited as a 'premise', one that is necessary for the writing of history. Marx reasons that

> ... we must begin by stating the first premise of all human existence and therefore, of all history, the premise, namely, that men must be in a position to live in order to be able to 'make history'. But life involves before everything else eating and drinking, a habitation, clothing and many other things. The first historical act is thus the production of the means to satisfy these needs, the production of material life itself. And indeed this is an historical act, a fundamental condition of all history, which today, as thousands of years ago, must daily and hourly be fulfilled merely in order to sustain human life... Therefore in any interpretation of history one has first of all to observe this fundamental fact in all its significance and all its implications and to accord it its due importance.[1]

The fate of the doctrine of historical materialism hangs on Marx's fundamental 'premise' that men and women work in order to survive, a statement that arrived like a thunderbolt in the Hegelian Germany of the 1840s. Social theory rapidly had to shift gears. It had to abandon the airy reaches of the human species' self-constitution in spirit in order to arrive at the earthly steppes of the laboring animal, one who fashioned the world, then became its object, only to become conscious of this dialectical detour and hopefully in the end to make the world once more, this time in a shape consonant with freedom.

Marx cautiously bestows upon his position the status of a 'premise' and regards the cognition of history as an act of 'interpretation'. At the epistemological level then, Marx's claim for his theory of history falls outside Descartes's absolutism, the quest for certainty. If historical materialism is not grounded on a claim to a truth superior to other theories of history, what then is the basis of its value? In *The*

German Ideology Marx does not attempt to justify his 'premise' or his "interpretation" in epistemological terms. He presents his view coherently, appealing to the reader to recognize its advantages. It is as if Marx were saying to the reader, 'Surely you cannot deny that human beings must labor in order to eat, clothe, and house themselves.' Once that postulate is granted Marx is content to go on and elaborate the concept of the mode of production, a concept which demonstrates that class struggles (and politics generally) derive from contradictions in the relations and forces of production. Still the original turn in Marx's argument to the 'premise' of labor remains little more than that, a premise.[2]

What is most surprising to me about Marx's relative silence on the issue of the labor premise is the strong contextual case that could have been made for it but was not. For in the mid-nineteenth century Western Europe was undergoing a great transformation precisely in the way men and women labored. The institution of the factory and its incorporation of steam power, all within a capitalist legal context, were altering drastically and therefore *making historical* the act of labor. Before the nineteenth century one could argue that labor was a constant, a relatively unchanging feature of the social landscape, unworthy of attention by historians because of its stagnant quality. That position was of course incorrect, but it was plausible. In the nineteenth century industrial capitalism was upsetting patterns that had endured for a thousand years, and its implication, as Marx noted well, was 'the automatic system' (automation) which might do away with manual labor altogether and inaugurate the 'realm of freedom' in place of the 'realm of necessity'.[3] For whatever motive, Marx chose not to bolster his argument on contextualist grounds and instead to present his analysis of industrial capitalism as the conclusion reached by his theory. And at that level one can examine the premise of labor as a possible source of limitation to the theory of historical materialism.

The premise of labor contains within it a Hegelian sub-premise: that the social field consists of subjects (laborers) and objects (matter), and that the interaction between the two results in the transformation of both. Marx, it is true, revises Hegel's position, insisting on the independence of the object and thereby resisting the Hegelian tendency to collapse the relationship of the two into the immanence of the subject. What interests us, however, is the way this subject-object relation limits the critical capacity of historical materialism. In a later moment of the theory it plays a crucial role in the determination of alienation and exploitation as the specific features of the capitalist system that require revolutionary transformation. In the instance of alienation, Marx's structural critique of capitalism contends that under this mode of production the subject-object relation is reversed.[4] The laborer becomes the object of the machine, as men and women lose control over the work process. Or, on another issue, human species' being is thwarted because the creative characteristics of the subject become subordinated to its objective, material need to survive. Human beings work in order to live, Marx complains, not in order to fulfill their creative potential; work is not enjoyment, realization, or satisfaction, but necessity and drudgery. Capitalism is in need of revolutionary criticism, Marx asserts, because it constitutes improperly the subject-object relation in the realm of work.

This critique from the *1844 Manuscripts* is echoed in *Capital* when Marx analyzes the commodity structure of labor. Under the capitalist mode of production the commodity form is generalized. Products are manufactured not for the use of the producers, but to be sold in markets. These products, or commodities, flow through the social system, taking on peculiar qualities and transforming relations between men and women. Marx is disturbed by the fact that under the commodity form, the subjective quality of labor is distorted:

> A commodity is therefore a mysterious thing, simply because in it
> the social character of men's labor appears to them as an objective
> character stamped upon the product of that labor; because the
> relation of the producers to the sum total of their own labor is
> presented to them as a social relation, existing not between them-
> selves, but between the products of their labor.[5]

Commodities are a source of concern to Marx because human
properties are invested in things, or become fetishized. The
object appears to be the subject. But what is worse is that
the reverse is also true: the subject appears to be the object.
Labor itself becomes a commodity, a thing. Just as there is,
under capitalism, a market for soy beans, so there is a market
for soy bean pickers. Work is subject to the double character
that all commodities have: it has a use value and an exchange
value. As a consequence, human qualities are evaluated in the
same terms that one uses to evaluate things.[6] Once again,
capitalism is faulted because subjects become objects, workers
become things.

The notion of exploitation derives from similar assumptions.
The worker-subject produces thing-objects for the capitalist
but does not receive back the proper amount of thing-objects
from the capitalist. Surplus value, created by worker-subjects
and stolen from them by capitalists, is the structural basis
of the capitalist system. It should be pointed out that the
current divergence between humanist and structuralist
Marxists does not affect the issue. Both positions fail to
question the labor premise. The structuralists attempt to
extricate Marxism from the subject-object relation, but they
do so at a later point in the theory. What remains unchallenged
is the premise that men and women labor and that they do
so by acting upon materials to produce objects.

The question that needs to be asked about Marx's premise
is this: is domination revealed best on the basis of consti-

tuting the social field as one in which men and women act on things? Another premise, one which constitutes the social field in quite another manner and which shall be defined below, would serve that function better. Besides, there is much reason to question the premise even if an alternative were not available. It cannot be taken for granted that human socieites are structured by the subject-object relation of labor, nor that change in society can best be understood by referring back to a subject who makes something, in this case a social change. On the contrary, there is reason enough to be suspicious. It can be argued, for example, that the model of subject acting upon object derives from the Judeo-Christian vision of creation, in which God acts upon (speaks to) matter and brings forth the Earth and its inhabitants as a finished product. The model of labor easily slips into a model of creation.

For a theory that calls itself historical *materialism*, a creationist model is suspect. The leanings towards aspects of idealism which Marx wants to avoid are strong in the subject-object dichotomy. In fact an immediate source for Marx's concept of labor was Hegel's discussion of the master–slave relation in the *Phenomenology of Mind*.[7] In that book the slave-worker represents human freedom not so much because he manipulates things, but because he establishes an idea of what he wants to make and then produces in the world a material artifact that represents that idea. The slave-worker in that way derives a sense of his powers, a confidence that his subjectivity can be the basis for the order of the world. The worker apprehends the force of his intellect and this is the basis for his freedom. Things operate much the same way in Marx's texts. One can argue that the 'materialism' of the labor premise is deceiving, that it has rather a loud note of idealism, that Marx celebrates and analyzes not the grime of the body's activity but the power of the mind over it. The entire analysis of the organization and exploitation of labor is subordinate, in one sense, to Marx's conviction that the subject's freedom to act upon its ideas is violated under the capitalist mode of production.

FOUCAULT'S PREMISE OF HISTORICAL MATERIALISM

Another premise available to historical materialism has been offered by Foucault. In this case the social field is constituted by a grid of technologies of power which act upon the body. It is assumed that there are human beings and things, but it is argued that the level of intelligibility pertinent to critical theory lies elsewhere, at the point where specific arrangements are located through which discourse/practices are created and constitute the social field as varying modes of domination. This alternative premise does not deny the existence of human beings and things, or their interaction, but it does maintain that the significant objects of investigation for historical materialism are arrangements in which the model of labor does not serve as the impetus of interpretation. The premise of technologies of power suggests that discourses and practices are intertwined in articulated formations having the domination of one group over another as their primary trait.[8] In addition, Foucault is able to focus his analysis on the body more directly than Marx. Because he is not looking for subjects and objects but for techniques of domination, Foucault is able to raise the question of the body more effectlively than Marx. He asks how the body is marked, positioned, temporalized, collected, and so forth, not so much how human beings have been degraded into things.

Suggestive as it is, the premise of technologies of power is not fully conceputalized in the works of Foucault and requires further theoretical elaboration. Even in a rough state, however, the premise is supported by an important contextual argument, one that has not received enough attention. If the Marxist premise of labor was bolstered, at least implicitly, by the dramatic change to industrial capitalism, that support has begun to evaporate in the advanced societies of the late twentieth century. Put quite simply, one can no longer assume as a basic paradigm of practice human beings working on things. The labor premise itself has been revolutionized as the factory system is increasingly marginalized. The United States, economists calculate, is the first service economy in world history. More than half of the working population is engaged neither in the primary sector (agriculture) nor the secondary (industry), but rather in the tertiary (service). This means that labor now takes the form of men and women acting on other men and women, or, more significantly, people acting on information and information acting on people. Especially in the advanced sectors of the economy, the manipulation of information tends to characterize human activity. Some economists argue that information workers do not characterize only the advanced sector but are in the majority overall.[9] The creation, transformation, and movement of information are the objects of most of the important new technologies that are introduced into the economy. We are told that very soon movement in the social field will involve information (electronically processed), not men or commodities. People will stay put while pulsations of electronic information will flow through social space.

If advanced capitalism is becoming an information society, in addition to the older configuration of a labor society, the labor premise can no longer be the first principle of critical theory. Domination cannot be theorized from the point of view of the labor activity, of the subject acting on matter to produce things. A new logic is called for that conceptualizes the social field on a different basis. And certainly one of the important features of the new premise must be that it accounts for the prominent place of information in the social space. I would maintain that Foucault's category of discourse/practice begins to meet the criteria for the new premise.

When discourse is theorized as the prominent feature of the social field, a new logic of domination is suggested, one that eschews the traits of the subject-object relation but follows rather the model of technologies of power. Historical materialism in the age of informational capitalism finds its premise in power that is the effect of discourse/practice. By the same token, the logic of discourse/practice finds its justification in the proliferation of information technologies. The value of the category discourse/practice can be demonstrated only in empirical studies.[10]

MARX'S DOCTRINE OF REASON

There are other premises in Marx's writings that poorly serve the interests of historical materialism. One in particular that needs criticism and revision is the notion of reason. Marx made very few statements about epistemology, leaving the impression that the development of revolutionary thought could proceed without extensive re-examination of existing (Hegelian?) doctrines of truth. In its assumptions about the nature of knowledge, critical theory was not, in Marx's eyes, substantially at variance with traditional theory. At least one can deduce this from Marx's silence. He did, it is true, offer one major innovation in epistemology. The eleventh 'Thesis on Feuerbach' states, 'The philosophers have only interpreted the world, in various ways; the point, however, is to change it.'[11] Since revolutionary theory is not simply interpretation but the basis for action, the criteria for truth cannot be limited to attributes of reason but must include judgements about the practical consequences incurred by it. Hence in the second 'Thesis on Feuerbach', Marx dismisses the epistemology of contemplative reason: 'The dispute over the reality or non-reality of thinking which is isolated from practice is a purely scholastic question.'[12] Given this distinction, Marx does not explore further the relation of thought to practice.

The first difficulty encountered with Marx's doctrine of reason is the assumption that the individual theorist can and should conceptualize the totality. In Marx's writings one cannot find the slightest hesitation on this question. He assumed as surely as he breathed that with the proper effort the intellectual can represent the real in conceptual terms. By the same token he takes it for granted that it is necessary to do this in order to develop revolutionary theory. At stake here is not the issue of the complexity of the world, a skepticism that would retreat from knowledge in modest homage to the ineffable mysteries of life. The issue is rather one of power, the power of discourse. By assuming that the totality is available to the theorist, Marx arrogates to his discourse and to his function as intellectual a kind of power that does not serve the interests of historical materialism. By fashioning itself as a theory of the totality, historical materialism ends in affirming the power of reason itself, appropriating for discourse the very revolutionary capacity it would attribute to the proletariat. In this sense, Marxism, although explicitly revolutionary, is implicitly a conservative doctrine tied to a traditional epistemological premise.

In the texts of Marx, the effects of this leviathan reason are at play and do their damage in numerous ways. A good example is the use of the notion of universality in relation to the working class. Before Marx, liberal theory attributed universality to democratic revolutions. When states were erected based on popular sovereignty, freedom would become universal. Universality was thus a political weapon in the hands of liberals in their battle against the 'partiality' of monarchical and aristocratic regimes. Liberals agitated for the freedom of all against the freedom of the one or the few. In the eighteenth and nineteenth centuries, political constitutions were drafted and put into effect which claimed universal freedom. Marx, of course, saw through the duplicity of liberal universalism. It was little more than a bourgeois device, perhaps well intended but then only self-deluding, to legitimate the hegemony of the capitalist class. The political emancipation of the liberals established the freedom of the bourgeoisie to exploit the proletariat.[13] Under the rule of representative democracy, the state became universal, but civil society remained divided into classes and subject to the domination of capital.

After effectively revealing the class interests at work in the liberal use of the notion of universality, Marx went on to apply the term in his own very different but still problematic manner. If the bourgeois revolution emancipated humanity only in the political sphere (and therefore only partially), the proletarian revolution would emancipate humanity in the social sphere and therefore totally. Complete emancipation is possible because factory workers, unlike the bourgeoisie, constitute a *universal* class. The classic statement of Marx's position is found in the *Contribution to the Critique of Hegel's Philosophy of Right: Introduction:*

> A class must be formed which has radical chains, a class in civil society which is not a class of civil society, a class which is the dissolution of all classes, a sphere of society which has a universal character because its sufferings are universal, and which does not claim a particular redress because the wrong which is done to it is not a particular wrong but wrong in general.[14]

The same statement is made again by Marx in *The German Ideology*, after the supposed epistemological break that Althusser thinks liberated Marx from Hegelian superstitions:

> This appropriation [of private property] is further determined by the manner in which it must be effected. It can only be effected through a union, which by the character of the proletariat itself can again only be a universal one, and through a revolution, in

which, on the one hand, the power of the earlier mode of production and intercourse and social organization is overthrown, and
on the other hand, there develops the universal character and the
energy of the proletariat, without which the revolution cannot be
accomplished.[15]

Factory workers are thus elevated from the plane of everyday
life and assume heroic proportions at the center of the world-
historical stage, upon which the drama of humanity's re-
demption is being enacted.

Reason indeed has its ruse, but not the one indicated by
Hegel. Marx wants to argue that factory workers are subjected
to a mode of domination which is difficult to comprehend
because it is not based on personal domination and is shrouded
in the liberal theory of the free contract. Surely he is correct:
alienation and exploitation are structural effects of the
capitalist mode of production. But that is not enough for
Marx. He insists on attributing to the oppression of factory
workers a universal suffering. He piles argument upon argument to make this case: the workers' suffering is universal
because men and women must eat before they can pray,
because they have no property and hence no private interests
to protect, because in the labor activity they subordinate
their life to their work, because the bourgeoisie has expanded
trade to a world scale and to overturn this system is to prepare for world-wide freedom, because automation is at the
heart of the industrial system promising the liberation of
human beings from toil, because labor is a commodity
stripping workers of their humanity, and so forth — all of
which is true but none of which proves the point about
universality.

A simple objection can be raised against the claim of
proletarian universality. Marx contends that only proletarians are capable of creating a classless society because
their subjugation is total, because they have nothing to
protect once they take power. Hence they have no interest

in domination. The bourgeoisie failed to establish a free society because it had an interest in protecting its property. Once it abolished aristocratic rule, it proceeded to erect new class divisions. Not so with the proletariat, Marx maintains. Yet Marx overlooked important considerations. Even the wretched state of the nineteenth-century factory worker was not devoid of interests in domination. The male proletarian had 'interests' in dominating his wife and children so that his revolution would be one that would perpetuate patriarchy and the authoritarian family. In this sense proletarians did not suffer 'wrong in general' and could not become the bearers of a universal revolution.

I do not know how this argument escaped Marx's attention, although it can be mentioned that in relation to his own family he was in many ways a typical bourgeois father. More significantly, this 'oversight' contributed to the systematic subordination of the questions of women's and children's oppression within socialist movements. It was easy to assume that once the universal class attained power, others' concerns would naturally be resolved. If we limit ourselves to the task of interpreting Marx's texts, however, an answer to the question appears at hand. Marx allowed himself to attribute more to the proletarian revolution than was warranted because of the assumption be held about the capacity of reason. His discourse appropriated the power to invest universality in the proletariat because he assumed that it was a legitimate function of the philosopher-theorist to make such judgements. Indeed such judgements were the stock in trade of the theorist. Countless thinkers in Western Europe and the United States were setting about the task of determining the nature of the universal. Marx was participating in a collective discourse in which it was taken for granted that reason could and should define the nature of the universal. Although his solution to the question was bold and original, it perpetuated a theoretical discourse which, far from enacting an epistemological break with the past, continued and even expanded the power of reason. At one level (the critique of the capitalist mode of production), Marx's discourse effects a critique of domination; at another level, it establishes and reinforces a mode of domination peculiar to discourse itself.

Emanicipatory discourse need not attribute the universal to a particular social group and it need not theorize the totality. When it does so, it conflicts with emancipatory practice in two important respects: (1) it removes from the popular forces the ability to define the limits and aims of practice, and (2) it gives the intellectual power over the liberation movement. The function of theory as 'guide' for practice becomes in the course of history the direct domination of theory over practice. The division of mental and manual labor in the capitalist mode of production is mirrored in the anti-capitalist movement as the intellectual becomes the brain and the proletariat the muscles of the revolutionary body.[16] By totalizing the social field in terms of the universal suffering of wage labor, Marx at the same time effected a closure which prevents other modes of domination from being named and analyzed. The epistemological problem for critical theory is thus not the one defined by Althusser, that is, to demonstrate the scientificity of Marx's theoretical revolution. It is rather a Kantian project of defining the limits of reason. The question is this, How can modes of domination be theorized and analyzed in such a way that the theorist does not appropriate more power than is necessary to carry out the theoretical function? If Foucault is right that discourses are always already powers, can a distinction be drawn between discourses whose powers strengthen existing modes of domination and those that work to undo them? If it is impossible adequately to define this epistemological distinction, it may at least be possible to enumerate aspects of critical theory which operate as modes of domination, such as Marx's use of the term 'universal'.

MARX'S USE OF THE DIALECTIC

Equally disturbing, from this perspective, is Marx's use of the dialectic to account for historical change. Discussions of the dialectic in Marx often hinge on the relationship with Hegel. Did Marx simply turn an idealist dialectic onto its materialist feet, or was the alteration more drastic in nature? Can a materialist kernel be extracted from an idealist husk, as another Marxist image of the relationship maintains? Was the Hegelian influence limited to the early Marx, or did it persist throughout his life? These questions have inspired much interest and produced a vigorous debate. For the present purposes, however, the issue of Hegelian influence can be bypassed and the discussion limited to an analysis of Marx's position.

In Marx's hands the broom of the dialectic was able to sweep away into the proverbial ashcan the commonplaces of liberal historiography. The dialectic gave a different shape to the past, presented a different explanation for the birth of the modern world, and foretold a different future for it. Historical change was not to be conceived as an incremental rise in the incidence of a given variable, such as scientific truth or gross national product. Nor was it to be seen as the emergence of an already existing natural property. Social systems, the dialectic taught, had internal contradictions. The seeds of their own destruction were inherent in their structure, specifically in the shape of class conflict. Historical change, therefore, was not the evolutionary rise of some feature of the social scene, but the complete transformation of society as a consequence of the contest of masters and slaves. History was not a continuous increase in law over arbitrary will, but a periodic, fundamental reshaping of systems of sanctions and restraints, to cite one example.

Liberal histories were populated by scientists and magicians, lawyers and tyrants, rational merchants and fanatical obscurantists all locked in a conflict that was traced to the dawn of time. The dialectic, on the contrary, revealed the inner transformation of both object and subject, without relying on fixed characters to perform the historical drama. Rather than a liberal vision of good and evil individuals, the dialectic established an image of humanity in a continual process of self-creation, with each set of characters emerging out of the past through a mechanism of opposition and transformation. Like the transformation of the slave in the chapters on Lordship and Bondage in Hegel's *Phenomenology*, social groups in Marx's dialectic were fundamentally different in each epoch. From the perspective of the dialectic, change was far more wide-ranging than liberal evolutionism would have it. The birth of industrial capitalism, for example, signified not simply a rise in living standards for manual laborers along with the institution of the labor contract. As Marx demonstrated, it included a new organization of labor, with tools and labor processes no longer at the disposal of the laborers. It meant, in short, the creation of a new social figure, the proletarian, who in no way resembled the artisan of the past even though he may have produced the same product.

In addition, the dialectic enabled Marx to show connections between phenomena that otherwise remained unrelated. Political revolutions and ideological changes were now illuminated by being related to changes at the social and economic level. Ideas no longer popped up inexplicably from the brain of some genius. Intellectual invention 'corresponded' to some aspect of social practice, without being determined mechanistically by it. The use of the dialectic permitted Marx to analyze historical phenomena that remained hidden from those wearing liberal spectacles. Above all, it enabled Marx to present a systematic critique of the existing social system, to reveal its transitory nature and to foresee a possible alternative course of historical transformation. The capitalist system was structurally flawed because it depended on a degraded type of labor which could not be ameliorated by improved material conditions. In that setting, representative democracy would be forced to operate in the interests of the capitalists against the workers. Scientific advances would serve not the integration of the human species and nature at a higher, more automated level, but would be limited by the constraints of the process of capital accumulation. Relations between the industrial and non-industrial worlds would involve not an equal exchange of surpluses but a brutal system of exploitation by the former.

In yet another way the dialectic provided Marx with an advantage over his liberal opponents. The dialectic not only conceptualized the historical field in a new way; it also transformed the nature of reason. In the *Critique of Dialectical Reason*, Sartre provides a comprehensive discussion of the difference between the analytical reason of liberalism and the dialectical reason of Marx.[17] Only one aspect of this difference needs attention here. The dialectic led Marx, against liberal presuppositions, to theorize from within the historical conjuncture. Marx explicitly adopted 'the point of view of the proletariat'. Reason was thus dependent upon the situation. For liberals, reason was a capacity inherent in human nature, one whose exercise was identical regardless of time or place. For Marx, reason was far less contemplative and deductive. It was bound to the task of the critique of domination and hence to the social field. Although the dialectic was not determined in a Lockean manner by sense impressions, it nonetheless prevented the theorist from adopting a vantage point outside time and space.

The theoretical advances of the dialectic are well known and cannot be effectively disputed. Nevertheless, significant difficulties remain unresolved by the dialectic, difficulties which are actually introduced by it. First there is a teleological momentum in the dialectic, a forward motion directed toward the resolution of social contradiction, even when historically no such movement exists. With a dialectical vantage point, the Marxist looks for and anticipates social agents who will recognize the contradiction and act upon that class consciousness. When such practice is not discovered by the historical materialist a negative term – false consciousness – is introduced, a term that does little to illuminate the specificities of the conjuncture. It is difficult for the dialectician to follow the sharp turns and sudden starts of historical events. In short, the dialectic is an over-ambitious concept that foresees too much, determines too much, and too easily fools the analyst into a false security. Armed with such a powerful analytic tool, the historical materialist falls into the habit of class analysis and becomes unwilling to seek out the unexpected.

Second, there is a homogenizing tendency in the dialectic. After all, Hegel's great ambition was a unified view of the real and the strategy of his dialectic was always to discover the connections between things, connections often lost in the humble procedures of Aristotelian logic. Historical materialism carries over this characteristic of the Hegelian dialectic, at times approaching a version of evolutionism. The application of the category of class struggle to different historical epochs introduces into the analysis an unwanted constancy. Subordinate classes always seem to oppose domination and ruling classes begin to look alike in the strategies they adopt to prevent revolution. At another level of analysis – that of the change from one mode of production to another – the same trend toward unity makes itself felt. Modes of production, from a dialectical vantage point, lead into one another to such an extent that the breaks and ruptures of history are smoothed over. Beneath the sound and fury of the class struggle, the logic of contradiction continues uninterruptedly, moving from one mode of production to another, each time approaching more closely the inevitable result – the classless society. Decades ago Merleau-Ponty complained that the dialectic does not allow for contingency.[18] One may add to that accusation that it does not allow for difference either.

If one goal of historical materialism is to demonstrate the transitory nature of practices and institutions, thereby avoiding an ideological justification of what is, a primary consideration must be to indicate that things were not always the way they are, that difference existed. But the dialectic moves by a logic of reconciliation or synthesis, bringing opposing forces together in a resolution that at once cancels and preserves their differences. Such a logic serves to domesticate the past, taming its strange and threatening features. The medieval chroniclers traced the glories of a noble lineage from the distant past to the present, celebrating each generation's contribution to the house. In different ways and to different degrees, liberal and Marxist historians resemble their medieval colleagues. In each case, the present age emerges as a culmination of the past, finding support in the sheer weight of bygone practices.

ALTERNATIVES TO THE DIALECTIC

Friedrich Nietzsche, that determined hater of his own age, developed an alternative historical logic.[19] Genealogy, as he termed it, was an effort to delegitimize the present by separating it from the past. The historian could depict the present as finite, limited, even repugnant, simply by locating differences in the past. The Nietzschean historian begins with the present and goes backward in time until a difference is located. Then he proceeds forward again, tracing the transformation and taking care to preserve the discontinuities as well as the connections in the historical line.

With the notion of difference as the guiding thread, historical materialists could open up the social field, unlocking the door of dialectical confinement. Instead of the search for totalized, universal suffering, historians could locate particular modes of domination, indicating the operations of technologies of power, as Foucault calls them, and tracing their lines of differential, discontinuous development. The rationalizations, justifications, and ideological niceties that mask practices of domination in the present could be revealed in juxtaposition to equally coherent, but very different, ideas and practices from the past. Foucault has provided this sort of analysis of the prison systems of the Old Regime and the nineteenth century; Ariès[20] and Gutman[21] have achieved similar analyses of family life in France and the American South. In each case, a specific mode of domination is analyzed, its ancient contours rendered comprehensible and juxtaposed by parallel, modern practices. In these analyses, the historical field is left open and reduced to the mode of domination in question. It is true, as Michel de Certeau points out,[22] that *Discipline and Punish* at times regresses to a totalizing logic in which the panopticon becomes the model for all forms of domination. But this must be considered a lapse in a study that attempts to set into play a Nietzschean logic of difference.

There is one place in the *German Ideology* where Marx reflects on the nature of his premises. In the section entitled 'Ideology in General, German Ideology in Particular', Marx distinguishes his own position from that of the various forms of contemporary Hegelianism. Hegelian philosophers, he argues, do battle against 'conceptions, thoughts, ideas', 'illusions', 'fantasies' – all the 'phrases' of the world. Unlike these quixotic warriors, he will take on reality itself. From the fact of having the real as his object, Marx deduces the epistemological certainty of his premises:

The premises from which we begin are not arbitrary ones, not dogmas, but real premises from which abstraction can only be made in the imagination. They are the real individuals, their activity and the material conditions under which they live, both those which they find already existing and those produced by their activity. These premises can thus be verified in a purely empirical way.[23]

THE LIMITATIONS OF HISTORICAL
MATERIALISM

With these fateful words, Marx opens the door to historical materialism and closes the door behind him on idealism. Historical materialism locates its beginnings in a double manoeuvre which splits discourse from practice and then subordinates the former to the latter. In that way he introduces a division in critical theory between what human beings say and what they do, a division which can no longer go unchallenged. By excluding mental operations from the domain of historical materialism, Marx remains within the traditional, Enlightenment metaphysic, only he favors its Lockean, sensationalist school. In the notebooks of historical materialists, impressions of labor activity can be recorded. Thus the critique of capitalism is 'verified in a purely empirical way'.

Unfortunately Marx's premises remain arbitrary as the distinction he draws between idealism and materialism preserves in a mirror image the metaphysic of liberalism. The problem is not, as Derrida thinks, that Marx privileges matter over idea because of the former's property of otherness.[24] In the *Theses on Feuerbach*, Marx defines his new type of materialism against the existing forms of idealism and materialism. He is interested not so much in the logical coherence of each position, as in the kind of field each opens up for historical investigation. Thus idealism can be rejected because it is concerned only with what men and women say, not with what they do. Materialism can be rejected because it constitutes its object as a passive determinant, forgetting 'that it is men who change circumstances'.[25] The conclusion Marx reaches is that historical materialism must combine the 'real' object as defined by materialism and the characteristic of activity as defined by idealism. The resulting historical materialism would have praxis as its object; that is to say, history would be constituted as class struggle, as human beings acting to change the world.

Without denying the advantages for critical theory of historical materialism as compared with liberal definitions of history, one can still not overlook the difficulties it contains. Historical materialism presumes an active subject who is ready to change the world and it privileges practice over discourse. In order to reconstitute historical materialism, it is necessary to proceed from different assumptions. Instead of an active subject, critical theory needs to constitute its object as modes of domination. Similarly, instead of 'real individuals', a category such as discourse/practice in Foucault avoids many of the hazards of giving priority to action over thought.

Historical materialism is not the opposite of historical idealism. In many respects the same premises are employed by historians of both liberal and Marxist stripes. The former write the history of politics, diplomacy, and ideas; the latter write the history of modes of production, social groups, and imperialism. Liberals narrate the past as evolution and record the moral acts of the hero, the individual subject; Marxists analyze social contradictions and register class conflicts, the collective subject. But this opposition is like that of Protestants and Catholics. Luther and Calvin broke the hegemony of the Papists and changed some doctrine, rituals, and organizational forms. In the end they still remained Christians just as Marxists remain children of the Enlightenment or humanists.

The texts of Marxist historians employ many of the categories and premises of the liberals. Both positions totalize the social field, presume the capacity of reason to grasp the real, search for causes of change and origins of phenomena, domesticate the past by tracing its continuity with the present, conceptualize the historical field through the subject-object dichotomy, and establish a human science in which theory governs practice, reason controls history, the intellectual dominates the movement of emancipation. Today, when the roles of the humanities and the social sciences are called into question, neither historical idealism nor historical materialism can provide the framework for critique. Once knowledge is implicated in power, Marxism like liberalism cannot escape the abuse of history.

With the limitations of classical Marxism clearly before us, we can turn to an examination of Foucault's proposals for developing a new kind of history, one that attempts to avoid the difficulties of both liberal and Marxist historiography. I will be interested in particular in establishing Foucault's credentials as an historian, in reviewing the categories he develops to provide an alternative to existing models, and in assessing the success of his position as a critical theory of the mode of information. As a reminder to the reader, let me state that I will be concerned primarily with his post-1968 works, books in which the critique of domination and the concept of power are central and therefore authorize an evaluation in relation to the problems developed by Western Marxists.

NOTES

1. Karl Marx, *The German Ideology*, in Robert Tucker (ed.), *Marx-Engels Reader* (New York: Norton, 1978), pp. 155–6.
2. See Gerald Cohen, *Karl Marx's Theory of History* (New York: Oxford University Press, 1978).
3. Marx, *Capital*, Vol. 3, in Tucker, *Marx-Engels Reader*, p. 441.
4. Marx, *1844 Manuscripts*, in Tucker, ibid., pp. 66–124.
5. Marx, *Capital*, Vol. 1, in Tucker, ibid., p. 320.
6. Georg Lukács, *History and Class Consciousness*, trans. R. Livingstone (London: Merlin, 1971).
7. G. F. W. Hegel, *Phenomenology of Spirit*, trans. A. V. Miller (New York: Oxford University Press, 1977).
8. For examples, see Michel Foucault, *Discipline and Punish*, trans. Alan Sheridan (New York: Pantheon, 1977).

9. Marc Porat, *The Information Economy: Volume 1, Definition and Measurement* (Washington, DC: Department of Commerce, 1977), p. 8.

10. Jacques Donzelot, *The Policing of Families* (New York: Pantheon, 1979).

11. Marx, *Theses on Feuerbach*, in Tucker, *Marx-Engels Reader*, p. 145.

12. Ibid., p. 144.

13. Marx, *The Jewish Question*, in Tucker, *Marx-Engels Reader*, pp. 26–52.

14. Cited in Tucker, *Marx-Engels Reader*, p. 64.

15. Cited in ibid., p. 192.

16. Rudolf Bahro in *The Alternative in Eastern Europe*, trans. David Fernbach (London: New Left Books, 1978), notes that Marx and Lenin attempted to resolve the lack of development among workers by giving theory a role in dominating the movement. See pp. 39ff.

17. Jean-Paul Sartre, *Critique of Dialectical Reason*, trans. Alan Sheridan-Smith (London: New Left Books, 1976), pp. 18–21.

18. Maurice Merleau-Ponty, *Sense and Non-Sense, Part II*, trans. Hubert and Patricia Dreyfus (Evanston: Northwestern University Press, 1964).

19. Friedrich Nietzsche, *The Use and Abuse of History*, trans. A. Collins (New York: Bobbs-Merrill, 1957), and *The Genealogy of Morals*, trans. W. Kaufman and R. Hollingdale (New York: Vintage, 1967).

20. Philippe Ariès, *Centuries of Childhood*, trans. Robert Baldick (New York: Vintage, 1965).

21. Herbert Gutman, *The Black Family in Slavery and Freedom, 1750–1925* (New York: Vintage, 1976).

22. Michel de Certeau, 'On the Oppositional Practices of Everyday Life', *Social Text*, 3 (Fall, 1980), pp. 23ff.

23. Marx, *The German Ideology*, in Tucker, *Marx-Engels Reader*, p. 149.

24. See the discussion of the issue with Jacques Derrida, in *Positions*, trans. Alan Bass (Chicago: University Press, 1981), pp. 60–67.

25. Marx, *Theses on Feuerbach*, in Tucker, *Marx-Engels Reader*, p. 144.

3

A New Kind of History

If the Marxist concept of labor cannot serve as the organizing principle of historical research, the question of an alternative theory becomes urgent. In this chapter I delineate the main features of Foucault's theory of history and assess its merits as a new general framework for historians.

In the past few decades the discipline of history has been revolutionized by new methodologies and new objects of study which fall under the rubric of 'social history'. Journals like the *Annales* in France and *Past and Present* in England have been the centers of the new concerns. Topics like population, the city, the family, women, classes, sports and psychobiography have risen to prominence over more traditional historical subjects. Methodologies have been imported from every social science: econometrics from economics, family reconstitution from demography, 'thick interpretation' from anthropology, voting analysis from political science, questionnaire analysis and class analysis from sociology, psychoanalysis from psychology. Once a field in the humanities relying on narrative writing, history has become a potpourri of social science methods. Not since Ranke's time has history undergone such dramatic revisions. Marxists have benefited from the new eclecticism as historical materialism has finally been accepted by the profession. Another index of the change is the new status of psycho-history. It was only a short time ago that Erik Erikson's masterful study of Martin Luther was spurned by historians, not even receiving a review in the *American Historical Review*. Today there are courses on psycho-history, journals of psycho-history and conferences at major universities on psycho-history.

It goes without saying that there is considerable confusion. A standard curriculum in history is a thing of the past. While there is much to be said for the intellectual vigor of the situation, it is also possible to conclude despairingly that the discipline is shattered into countless splinters and will never again take on a recognizable shape. It may instead be absorbed by the individual social sciences as an ornament to their own concerns. A major reason for the incoherence of historical writing today is the absence of theoretical reflection by the practitioners of social history. Marxist historiographers are, one would think, an exception, since their writing derives from a well-articulated theoretical tradition. Yet that is not always the case. One of the most prominent Marxist historians, Edward Thompson, looks upon theory with no more understanding than does his cat, to judge from his recent revealingly titled polemic against Althusser, *The Poverty of Theory* (1978). While Thompson's anti-theoretical animus is not shared by all Marxist historians, a major tendency in their writing is to adopt empiricist positions only bolstered by a strong political commitment to socialism. The non-Marxist social historians are for their part even more adamant in ignoring the theoretical presuppositions of their work. A large segment of them simply adopt a quantitative methodology and pursue the facts defined by the method, never examining the conceptual parameters of the field constituted by that method. Thus in Peter Laslett's writing, family history is reduced to the number of blood relations residing in the same household. Since statistical precision is required, questions about family life that are not quantifiable become irrelevant and are suppressed. In general, However, among social historians, methodological purity does not suppress intellectual curiosity and the new tendencies must be regarded with favor.

Nevertheless, despite clear advances, the opportunity raised by social history to question the basic assumptions of the field constituted by historical investigation has gone unrecognized.[1] The mere variety of topics pursued by historians today encourages a rigorous examination of the theoretical assumptions of the field. If family history, urban history, women's history and environmental history are all valid fields of investigation, what are the principles by which one chooses to do one or the other? How is the social field being constituted by each tendency? Do the objects of investigation in each one bear any relation to those of the others? Are they in contradiction or can they somehow be collected together as a general history? These questions are only the beginning of a theoretical examination of social history that is much needed today. The virtue of the recent writings of Foucault is that by their very difference from social history they raise the important theoretical questions in the most forceful way.

The flow of Foucault's texts, the way one thing is put after another, disturbs the expectations of the reader familiar with social history. There appear to be huge gaps in the narrative, silences that scream at the reader. Topics are annoyingly placed out of the normal order, disrupting one's sense of logical sequence. Levels of analysis are mixed together in irritating confusion: the difference between ideas and behavior goes unrecognized and is violated. Simple questions of causality are ignored or appear in reverse order. The writing is thick and metaphoric and the point of view of the narrative line is often lost. The object of investigation is never quite clarified and appears to be neither individuals, nor groups, nor institutions. What is worse, things seem to shift in the course of the writing; at the beginning one issue is at stake, by the end we seem to be reading about something else. Worst of all, the author's attitude toward the topic of study never emerges clearly. He seems to take a perverse pleasure in shifting his stance, or simply in adopting provocatively an unorthodox attitude toward a topic. Finally, while much research has contributed to Foucault's studies, a great deal of material has not been looked at. The evidential basis of the texts is odd and incomplete. No wonder historians are skeptical about the value of his efforts.

Although Foucault's work is read by anthropologists, sociologists, psychologists, philosophers, literary critics, and historians, the basic impact of his work is historical. Foucault offers a new way of thinking about history, writing history, and deploying history in current political struggles. If Foucault is the *enfant terrible* who would destroy the human sciences, he is also one of their most fascinating practitioners, reshaping their contours according to an original if most peculiar historical practice. Foucault is an anti-historical historian, one who in writing history, threatens every canon of the craft. One can ask, therefore, if there is a theory of history in Foucault's texts. Can one discover, against the grain of Foucault's anti-systematic writing, a set of concepts or categories that reveals the basis of his powerful and shocking accomplishments?

A reading of Foucault's major writings might lead one to conclude that Foucault has not developed anything like a theory of history. He has written no Toynbeean study of the past encompassing the last few millennia in a schema of categories. He has written no theory of causation to argue that one factor or set of factors directs human destiny. He has written no teleological tract to prove that the meaning and future of mankind will be realized in a given manner. Moreover, practising historians in the English-speaking world for the most part will not even grant that Foucault is one of their own. Many American and British historians have received Foucault's books not as the development of a new theory of history and not even as the work of an empirical historian, but rather as an attack on the discipline of history. One historian notes in passing Foucault's extreme 'dismissal of the intrinsic value of the discipline of history'.² Another historian, writing in the prestigious *Journal of Modern History*, spends fifty pages warning historians of the dangers of Foucault's writing for their craft.³ By what right then can one speak of Foucault's theory of history?

It must be recalled that Foucault held a chair in history (History of the Systems of Thought) at the Collège de France until his untimely and tragic death. It must also be mentioned that Foucault has written a half dozen books that concern aspects of the European past. *Madness and Civilization* (1961), *The Birth of the Clinic* (1963), *The Order of Things* (1966), *The Archeology of Knowledge* (1969), *Discipline and Punish* (1975), and *The History of Sexuality* (1976) are all at least superficially works of history. How can it be that someone who has studied the past so productively is not granted the title historian?

THE THESIS OF DISCONTINUITY

The answer, it would appear, is clear: Foucault does not narrate the evolution of the past; he does not tell the story of how 'the seamless web of yesteryear' leads slowly and inexorably into the present. In short, Foucault is not an historian of continuity but of discontinuity. Foucault attempts to show how the past was different, strange, threatening. He labors to distance the past from the present, to disrupt the easy, cozy intimacy that historians have traditionally enjoyed in the relationship of the past to the present. He strives to alter the position of the historian from one who gives support to the present by collecting all the meanings of the past and tracing the line of inevitability through which they are resolved in the present, to one who breaks off the past from the present and, by demonstrating the foreignness of the past, relativizes and undercuts the legitimacy of the present. And Foucault does this bluntly, even abrasively, as in this example where he chides intellectual historians for their obsession with the filiation of ideas, a variation of the continuity thesis:

> ... to seek in this great accumulation of the already-said the text that resembles 'in advance' a later text, to ransack history in order to rediscover the play of anticipations or echoes, to go right back to the first seeds or to go forward to the last traces, to reveal in a work its fidelity to tradition or its irreducible uniqueness, to raise or lower its stock of originality, to say that the Port-Royal grammarians invented nothing, or to discover that Cuvier had more predecessors than one thought, these are harmless enough amusements for historians who refuse to grow up.[4]

The maturation of the historian thus requires the acquisition of the taste for the past as a penchant for what is different.

Foucault unmasks the epistemological innocence of the historian. He raises the discomforting question: What does the historian do to the past when he or she traces its continuity and assigns it its causes? For Foucault, history is a form of knowledge and a form of power at the same time; put differently, it is a means of controlling and domesticating the past in the form of knowing it. The historian pretends to recreate the past, in Ranke's phrase, as it really was. Using an awkward combination of anecdote and statistic, the historian paints the landscape of the past in the colors of the present. He or she explains the present by the past, *claiming the disclosure* of the truth or a truth about both. The historian accomplishes this goal without placing himself or herself in question. Instead, the historian's work is motivated by the sheer force of truth, the quest for knowledge.

Let us not misunderstand what is at stake. Foucault's critique is not based on the opposition of objectivity and relativity, of science and ideology. His position may sound similar to the attack on value neutrality, but something else is in question. It would not help, for example, if the historian were to acknowledge openly his values: love of country, party advocacy, or the like. Foucault's critique is more basic than this. Whether one writes history under the guise of objectivity, or for the explicit purpose of an ideological cause, is not the heart of the matter. Instead, what is at issue is the act of an individual claiming to contain within his or her conciousness a certain truth about the past and representing it in writing. Foucault does not claim that such an effort is impossible or illegitimate, but that this operation is an active, willful working on materials. It is a creation, a fiction, in the full sense of the term, one which, as it has been practiced by positivists, liberals, and Marxists alike, produces a discourse with a set of meanings that acts upon everyone who comes into contact with it. Historical writing, Foucault contends, is a practice that has effects, and these effects tend, whatever one's political party, to erase the difference of the past and justify a certain version of the present. And finally, the practice of the discourse of the past places the historian in a privileged position: as the one who knows the past, the historian has power. The historian becomes an intellectual who presides over the past, nurtures it, develops it, and controls it. Since, under the thesis of continuity, the historian is able to collect within himself or herself the experience of the past, he or she has an ideological interest in maintaining its importance, reasserting the inevitability with which the past leads to the present, while at the same time denying that there is a certain power at stake. Foucault writes:

> Continuous history is the indispensable correlative of the founding function of the subject: the guarantee that everything that has eluded him may be restored to him; the certainty that time will disperse nothing without restoring it in a reconstituted unity; the promise that one day the subject — in the form of historical consciousness — will once again be able to appropriate, to bring back under his sway, all those things that are kept at a distance by difference, and find in them what might be called his abode.[5]

In this way history, as presently practiced, enacts an Hegelian totalization of the past and the present.

Foucault's critique of the epistemology of historical practice is clarified and reveals its importance when it is brought to bear on those historical schools that present themselves consciously as advocates of progress. When the relationship is made explicit between the writing of history and the movement of liberation in the present, the force of Foucault's thesis of discontinuity becomes apparent and appears most appropriate. The Marxist school of historiography is the most fruitful example. According to the tenets of historical materialism, there is a direct relationship between theory and historical writing on the one hand and the movement for social emancipation on the other. The investigation of class conflicts under the aegis of the theory of the mode of production is a guide for the conduct of the struggle in the present. History, for Marxists, is written neither for amusement nor for self-cultivation. One writes history in order to promote revolution. Class struggles of the past, however diverse their characters, are gathered by these historians and confirm the movement of social liberation in the present. Hence the continuity of the past and the present is maintained. The Marxist historian is no mere curator of a museum of forgotten struggles but, by virtue of his or her knowledge, a privileged participant in the present situation of revolt. The theoretically informed historian knows more than the workers about the strategy for change. Marxism thereby sanctions a certain type of intellectual to represent the workers in the task of revolution. Leninism finds its support in historical materialism, receiving power over the workers by dint of the intellectuals' ability to know the past and therefore the present. The truth of the movement for social transformation is removed from the hands of the workers and transferred into the minds of the intellectuals. History has been abused, according to the Foucauldian thesis, as the doctrine of continuity has allowed the struggle of the workers to be appropriated by the intellectuals.

The intention of this argument is not to single out Marxists

and condemn their errors, as anti-Communist cold warriors
might suppose. The same analysis could be given of liberal
historians, positivists, and even that most recalcitrant of all
groups, empiricists. In fact, since empiricists still dominate
historical writing in the United States and Britain, they are
the ones most in need of critical examination. Nevertheless,
I will explore Foucault's theory of history further by continuing to interrogate Marxism, because that school of historiography is, I believe, the most important and because
Foucault himself, situated in France, is concerned most
directly with it.

KNOWLEDGE/POWER

In the 1970s Foucault produced two books, *Discipline and
Punish* and *The History of Sexuality*, which initiated something of a new departure from his earlier writings and developed significantly his theory of history. In the books on
prisons and sexuality, his aim is to explore a configuration of
knowledge and power, or a set of configurations, that have
become increasingly characteristic of twentieth-century
European and American society. He argues that knowledge
and power are deeply connected and that their configuration
constitutes an imposing presence over advanced industrial
society, extending to the most intimate recesses of everyday
life. The form of domination characteristic of advanced
capitalism is not exploitation, not alienation, not psychic
repression, not anomie, not dysfunctional behavior. It is
instead an new pattern of social control that is embedded
in practice at many points in the social field and that constitutes a set of structures whose agency is at once everyone
and no one.

   In the last chapter I analysed Marx's concept of labor,
pointing out its theoretical limitations. At this point I will
restate some of those objections, placing them in the context

of Foucault's critique of the subject and indicating why they appear, from Foucault's perspective, similar to liberal assumptions about history. I will then show how the concept knowledge/power, Foucault's alternative to the category of the laboring subject, is able to illuminate the historical field in a promising manner. I will then go on to discuss the Western Marxist categories of ideology and repression. From a Foucauldian perspective, these ideas are also flawed in their application to historical discourse.

According to Foucault and several radical theorists who present an associated line of argumentation (Gilles Deleuze, Félix Guattari, Jean Baudrillard, Jean-François Lyotard), Marx's concept of labor is flawed by its reliance on aspects of liberal theory which it seeks to transcend. The concept of labor as developed by Marxists and liberals alike constitutes the social world as the product of a collective subject, the work force. Marxists then show how the products of labor are stolen from the worker-subject by the mechanisms of exploitation and alienation. For liberals, the worker receives a just wage, determined by the market, so that domination is eliminated. In both cases, however, the question of historical–social analysis centers on the subject. For liberals, the drama reaches its crisis when the contract is made: two subjects, acting rationally, agree to mutual obligations. For Marxists, the script is varied at one level and the same at another: worker-subjects act upon matter, creating things that circulate through the channels of the social world. But even here we have the somewhat theological drama of active subjects shaping matter into desired forms. In both cases the social-historical field is available for analysis from the point of view of subjects.

For Foucault, these analyses are inadequate and Marxism cannot be the basis for a critical theory of history, because the modes of domination in the twentieth century cannot be perceived from the limited vantage point of the subject. Instead, domination today takes the form of a combination or

structure of knowledge and power which is not external to
the subject, but still unintelligible from his or her perspective.
Critical theory cannot present history as the transition from
abusive aristocrats to exploiting capitalists, because domination is no longer centered in or caused by subjects. The result
is that the labor process, as theorized by Marx, does not make
intelligible sources of radicalism that are adequate to overturning current modes of domination.

The point is not that the labor process is free of oppression
or of the prevailing 'technologies of power'. It is rather that
the shift to the new critical concepts is carried out better by
reference to other social practices — in part because Marxism
has colonized the category of labor, in part because the dominant structures have developed elsewhere. In the practices of
punishment and sexuality, in the social locations of the
family, the military, and the asylum, Foucault uncovered the
birth and development of new modes of domination, com-
binations of discourses and practices that constituted new
forms of subjugation. This process also affected labor practices under capitalism but not in the way Marx conceived it.
The discipline of the factory must not be equated with the
mechanisms of exploitation and alienation.

In *Discipline and Punish* and *The History of Sexuality*
Foucault divides the histories of crime and sex into two or
three main periods, with the eighteenth century serving as
one of the dividing lines. In the earlier periods, knowledge
and power about crime focused on the body of the trans-
gressor. In the exemplary but not representative case of the
regicide Damiens, 'technologies of power' were exercised to
extract the 'truth' of the crime by a complex of secret torture
and public punishment. Damiens's body became the target of
the knowledge/power of the judicial apparatus of the Old
Regime. His brutal public execution was the final ritual
through which the pre-modern system of punishment was
fulfilled.[6]

Before the Counter Reformation knowledge/power over

sexuality also concerned the body, its acts, and its trans-
gressions.[7] In this case, the discourse about sexuality was
governed by clerical, not secular authorities. The confessional
was the place where sexual acts were examined, discussed,
and evaluated. Questions were aimed at determining what
was done, by whom, in what positions, and how many times.
A fixed schedule of penances was elaborated over time to
regulate atonements for violations of the rules. In the pre-
modern period, then, knowledge/power created and shaped
practices of criminality and sexuality through manipulations
of the body, rearranging it when necessary to produce and
reproduce the social order. The full impact of Foucault's
analyses of these technologies of power requires a careful
reading of his texts. But the rough outlines of his discoveries
should be clear even from this brief account.

The early modern period is separated from the nineteenth
century and its unique structure of knowledge/power by a
dramatic discontinuity. In the more recent period, discourses
about sexuality and technologies of power over crime change
dramatically. Crime and sex become subjects of new disciplinary authorities that enact an extraordinary 'microphysics
of power', extending throughout the social landscape. Regarding crime, Bentham's *Panopticon* becomes one of the sources
for a new prison system; and for sexuality, Freud's theory of
repression eventually comes to govern the life of the family.[8]
In both cases new regimes are established in which convicted
criminals and sexual activity (especially of children) are
scrupulously monitored. The object of control has shifted
from the body to the mind, and the methods of control have
been extensively articulated as the effects of the technologies
of power constitute new types of subordinated groups.
Elaborate bureaucracies are established to keep tabs on people;
extensive files are developed with an enormous expansion of
disciplines and scientific experimentation to study, examine,
and probe the most banal thoughts and actions of potential
criminals and recidivists, childhood masturbators and hysteri-

cal women. The elaboration of institutionalized discourses and powers is endless. Eventually, the population can be put under surveillance and observed almost continuously, like an amoeba under a microscipe. Although not every social institution adopted the model of the panopticon, its dissemination, as described by Foucault, was awesome:

> ... there was a whole series of mechanisms that did not adopt the 'compact' prison model, but used some of the carceral methods: charitable societies, moral improvement associations, organizations that handed out assistance and also practised surveillance, workers' estates and lodging houses.... And, lastly, this great carceral network reaches all the disciplinary mechanisms that function throughout society.[9]

In the instances of crime and sex studied by Foucault, the exercise of knowledge/power cannot be comprehended under the sign of repression. Sex was not repressed in the nineteenth century, as Freudo-Marxists would have us believe.[10] That is not the way technologies of power operate. On the contrary, Foucault points out that discourses on sex flourished in the nineteenth century as never before. If overt sexuality passed under a ban in polite society of the Victorian era, that is only because it had become more, not less, of a preoccupation. In bourgeois families, parents studied the new medical literature on child rearing which warned them of the dangers of masturbation. A combined operation both denied childhood sexuality and marshaled parents' energies against it. Sexuality was elicited from children and then subjected to extensive rules to prevent its overt manifestation. Similarly, the classic hysterical woman was considered to contain a bundle of sexually contradictory impulses and, at the same time, was idealized as a vessel of purity and innocence. In these instances, there was not an activity which was 'repressed', but an extensive development of knowledge/power which shaped, constituted, and controlled practices according to complex rules. Hand in hand, technologies of power and discourses are, according to Foucault, positive, creative forces, not negative, preventive measures.

If this is so, how can one explain the widespread belief, one not limited to the Freudo-Marxists, that power is something that denies, forestalls, represses, prevents? In one of his numerous interviews, Foucault provides a highly suggestive hypothesis to account for the view that power is negative.[11] The Western system of law, he argues, was developed in the context of the monarchical system. As the kings established themselves as centers of power, they were opposed successively and at times concurrently by the nobility and the bourgeoisie. The nobility sought to regain rights and liberties which the monarch denied them, as in the Magna Carta, and the bourgeoisie generated a system of law which aimed at curtailing, limiting, and preventing actions of the monarch which were injurious to the instauration of a market economy. The monarch prevented private feuds among aristocrats and bourgeois law abolished the arbitrary abuses of kingship. In both cases what was at stake was a conception of power as negative or repressive. Over the centuries, the practices and discourses concerning power have thought of it only in this way. Since power is actually positive, the view that it is negative functions as an ideology masking its acutal nature.

THE CONCEPT OF IDEOLOGY

Just as the concept of repression deriving from the Freudian tradition is inadequate as a guide to the workings of power, so the concept of ideology in the Marxist tradition fails to provide a theoretical compass to the historical manifestations of knowledge and discourse. Before examining Foucault's critique of the concept of ideology, I must explain its importance to the continuing vitality of Marxist theory. In the twentieth century, Marxist theorists in Italy, France, and

Germany have turned increasingly to the concept of ideology to account for various phenomena of advanced capitalism. Antonio Gramsci and Georg Lukács, the Frankfurt School, Jean-Paul Sartre and Louis Althusser have all resorted to the notion of ideology to explain, within a Marxist framework, important cultural transformations that have apparently delayed the progress of proletarian revolution. The role of nationalism in defusing class conflict in times of war, the role of race in dividing the working class, the role of consumerism in purchasing workers' allegiance to capitalism, the role of the educational system and the media in transforming contradiction into consent, the role of the family in providing an escape from the battle over the means of production — all these have insured that the ideas of the ruling class shall remain the ruling ideas. The concept of ideology thus occupies a crucial position in the apparatus of Marxism, explaining how class consciousness slips continuously into false consciousness. If the concept of ideology is undermined and found wanting, Marxists might be hard put to present a coherent account of the relative absence of class struggle in the advanced societies.

Foucault presents the following critique of the concept of ideology:

The notion of ideology appears to me to be difficult to use for three reasons. The first is that, whether one wants it to be or not, it is always in virtual opposition to something like the truth. Now I believe that the problem is not to make the division between that which, in a discourse, falls under scientificity and truth and that which falls under something else, but to see historically how truth-effects are produced inside discourses which are not in themselves either true or false. The second inconvenience is that it refers, necessarily I believe, to something like a subject. Thirdly, ideology is in a secondary position in relation to something which must function as the infrastructure or economic or material determinant for it. For these three reasons, I believe that it is a notion that one cannot use without precautions.[12]

Foucault's first objection to the concept of ideology addresses the binary opposition of science/ideology that holds a prominent place in Marxist thought, especially Althusser's.[13] Ideology is conceived here as a form of mystification that does not attain the status of knowledge or science. To study ideology is thus to study ideas that thave been distorted through contamination with some aspect of relations based on domination, as in Habermas's notion of the ideal speech situation.[14] From Foucault's Nietzschean perspective, however, all discourses are merely perspectives, and if one has more value than another that is not because of its intrinsic properties as 'truth', or because we call it 'science', but because of an extra-epistemological ground, the role the discourse plays in constituting practices. By designating itself 'science', Marxism gives itself a false and easy legitimacy, one that enables the Marxist theorist to place himself or herself above the masses as the bearer of the universal. As a science, Marxism becomes just one more discourse that functions to generate a subjugated practice. Thus Foucault contends that the concept of ideology is but one more example of the way reason comes to dominate the very object it intends to liberate: man.

Foucault's second objection to the concept of ideology derives from his anti-humanism. The notion of ideology places the source of 'ideas' in subjects, such as the ruling class which, as the phrase from Marx goes, expresses the ruling ideas of every age. The reference back to the subject prevents one from examining ideas in the manner preferred by Foucault, as discourses whose intelligibility does not derive from subjects. Foucault's anti-subjectivism is one of the guiding threads in his writings, which on other issues changed considerably from the 1960s to the 1970s. This tendency, it must be acknowledged, derives from the structuralist view of language as a decentered totality. Language for the structuralists is not a tool for the expression of the subject's ideas but a system of relations between signs which constitute its object as the subject. Foucault has consistently denied allegiance to structuralism,[15] which is accurate since he is not a formalist, pursuing a universal combinatory in the manner of Claude Lévi-Strauss.

Foucault's animus against the subject is motivated by his project to analyze the mechanisms of the human sciences. The disciplines which take 'man' as their object also have 'man' as their 'subject'. This hermeneutic circle produces a certain blindness which allows the human sciences to avoid reflecting upon their effects on practice. Foucault thinks that, by taking a point of view other than that of the subject, one can decipher the mechanisms through which the human sciences come to dominate, not liberate, the subject. His effort to develop the concept of discourse is motivated by this intention. Thus he defines discourse in opposition to the subject as follows:

> I shall abandon any attempt . . . to see discourse as a phenomenon of expression – the verbal translation of a previously established synthesis; instead, I shall look for a field of regularity for various positions of subjectivity. Thus conceived, discourse is not the majestically unfolding manifestation of a thinking, knowing. speaking subject, but, on the contrary, a totality, in which the dispersion of the subject, and his discontinuity with himself may be determined.[16]

Such a non-subjectivist concept of discourse invalidates the Marxist notion of ideology in its complicity with expressivist assumptions. The concept of ideology is inadequate for decoding the dimensions of domination inherent in the human sciences, disciplines which are ubiquitous today.

The third objection to the concept of ideology, that ideas are reducible to the mode of production, is found in Foucault's insistence upon the immanent relation of knowledge and power. Perhaps more than Marx, Foucault lays the basis for a materialist history of knowledge, since he conceives of ideas in such close proximity to practice. Discourses, for Foucault, are already powers and do not need to find their material force somewhere else, as in the mode of production. Most significantly for a critical theory of history, such a perspective shifts the focus of attention away from the sublime ideas of the intellectual elite and toward the mundane discourses of disciplinary institutions that more directly affect the everyday life of the masses. Ideology is no longer seen as the airy dialogue of great minds, but as the prosaic encounter of criminal and criminologist, neurotic and therapist, child and parent, unemployed worker and welfare agency.

Foucault is therefore opposed to a central doctrine of historical materialism upon which the concept of ideology rests: the distinction between the base and the superstructure. To the extent that Marxism depends upon this distinction, it can no longer serve as the primary basis for radical theory. Some Marxists defend their position by resorting to a concept of mediations, developed most extensively by Sartre in *Critique of Dialectical Reason*. The notion of base/superstructure, these Marxists contend,[17] is a relic of the Second and Third Internationals, no longer to be taken seriously by Marxists. Contemporary Marxists account for so-called superstructural levels, recognizing the mutual impact of base and superstructure. The old economic determinism of the 1920s and 1930s is dead. Marx and Engels themselves, it can be pointed out, denied such reductionism and warned their followers against it. While it can be admitted that the notion of mediations is an improvement over reductionism, it must also be noted that the improvement does not go far enough. The perspective of the reciprocal relations of base and superstructure is still unable to account for the internal complexity of any aspect of the 'superstructure' and remains tied to a totalizing impulse that Foucault finds problematic.

A MULTIPLICITY OF FORCES

Instead of refurbishing Marxism with a more complex method of totalization, Foucault proposes a multiplicity of forces in any social formation, a multiplicity which is dispersed, discontinuous, and unsynchronized. Social theory for him cannot grasp an entire social formation in one key concept or schema. It must rather explore each discourse/practice separately, unpacking its layers, decoding its meanings, tracing its development wherever its meandering path may lead. Foucault is an ardent detotalizer, preferring a syncopated approach which never pretends to capture the whole of a historical moment. He goes so far in this direction as to acknowledge, in some places, a perchant for pluralism.[18] In good part because Marxism (as well as liberalism) has so inured us to the habit of totalizing, the urgent need today is for shattering those great generalities — the rise of the bourgeoisie, the emergence of democracy, the class struggle, the capitalist mode of production — which for so long have dominated historical thinking. Foucault asks, What is the fear that leads to such hasty totalization? In place of 'global history' he would put 'general history', in which the aim would be to 'describe the peculiarity of practices, the play of their relations, the form of their dependencies'.[19]

In this spirit the emphasis in *Discipline and Punish* and *The History of Sexuality* is on the multiplicity and dispersion of knowledge and power, an emphasis which enacts a shift from the earlier notion of the episteme. In *The Order of Things*, for example, the episteme functioned as the master key to all discourses, even if Foucault did not intend it as such, and history was a succession of epistemes. Each age had its unique episteme which was the ground of all utterances. The episteme operated as a totalizing concept which rendered Foucault defenseless against the common attack that he could not explain the change from one episteme to another.

The substitution of the idea of a multiplicity of discourses/ practices for the episteme allows Foucault to escape from the problems of causation and change. Now Foucault can deal with the birth of prisons by incorporating the notion of discontinuity into a properly historical analysis, one that can follow changes where they occur and still put the stress on discontinuity. He can show first how the panopticon system breaks drastically with the past and second how it incorporates aspects of earlier disciplinary modes, such as the technology of power developed in the military to regiment large bodies of men and later transferred to the prison system. There can, in a Foucauldian analysis, be specific causes for specific changes, and continuities of particular types without losing the main argument that discontinuity is the central focus of historical research.

Foucault's recent writings also avoid the charge of ahistorical structuralism by incorporating notions of archeology and genealogy. Although these concepts remain somewhat unclear and imprecise in Foucault's texts, they do initiate a shift to an historical problematic that promises to strengthen his position vis-à-vis Marxism and traditional historiography. At the most general level, archeology and genealogy are morphological strategies, searching out the changing structure of diverse phenomena. Foucault uses the term archeology to denote a level of the analysis of discourses which grasps their "rules of formation" without reference to the subject.[21] The term genealogy implies the political function in which history is 'the reversal of a relationship of forces'.[22] The historian can undermine the present order by reversing its images of the past. The method advocated by Foucault requires the historian to go back in time until a difference is located, such as the torture of Damiens, the pre-Tridentine confessional, the medieval ship of fools. These alien discourses/practices are then explored in such a way that their negativity in relation to the present explodes the 'rationality' of phenomena that are taken for granted. When the technology of power of the past is elaborated in detail, present-day assumptions which posit the past as 'irrational', are undermined.

AN ALTERNATIVE TO MARX

This chapter has discussed the broad outlines of Foucault's recipe for writing history. In the subsequent chapters I will examine in more detail two of his texts, *Discipline and Punish* and *The History of Sexuality*. Before going on to those analyses I want to pause in order to clarify an especially difficult problem, i.e., the precise relationship of the theories of Foucault and Marx.

It is tempting to maintain that Foucualt simply replaces Marx as the master theorist of history. Some readers might in fact come to that conclusion if they were convinced by the above discussion. Yet that it not my intention, nor is it my judgement. Foucault's discourse analysis, whatever its merits, cannot replace class analysis or even liberal analyses of political and intellectual events. The issues fall at two distinct levels which require separate judgements about the impact of Foucault's work: (1) the general level of an historical framework and (2) the level of particular, monographic historiography.

Foucault's work is most threatening to Marxism at the general level. As a totalizing framework that encompasses all history in an evolutionary scheme and relates all levels of society under the dominance of the mode of production, Marxism cannot be sustained. The limitations of this kind of totalizing thought have already been discussed and need not be repeated here. Suffice it to say that Foucault's case is strongest in arguing for detotalizing historical theory. His critique of the subject is sustained both at the level of the object of historical investigation (the laboring subject in Marx) and the authorial subject who writes history. To repeat, the point of view of any particular subject (proletariat, democratizing politican, rational individual) is an inadequate basis for a totalization of the social field. At the same time the writer of an historical text employs a theoretical framework which is always partial, always limited in the field that it illuminates and therefore can never serve as an exclusive, all-encompassing foundation for historical theory. Since knowledge is always tied to power, the special position of the author of an historical text must always limit the scope of his or her claim to truth.

Once the pretensions of Marxism to serve as a totalizing historical theory are put to rest, it is then possible to assess the value of class analysis for particular historical objects. At this level Foucault's position does not at all exclude Marxist historical analysis. At this level the relative merits of Foucault's genealogy, Marxist class analysis and Whig history to illuminate the social-historical field need to be assessed in each particular case. At this level of the conflict of interpretive schemes, the merits of Foucault's position can be judged on the basis of how one envisages the needs of the present situation. If one is convinced that open public debate and parliamentary democracy are the fundamental requirements of the present situation, then Habermas's evolutionary linguistics or liberal political analysis provides the key indices of historical analysis. If one is convinced that the struggles of the working class are the center of the contemporary drama, then the Marxist position receives priority for historical work. If one is convinced that a new social formation is emerging in the advanced societies (the mode of information) in which knowledge is increasingly implicated in modes of domination and in which protest has shifted its focus away from the process of production, then Foucault's schema is the urgent item on the historiographical agenda. In any case, however, each position will be able to illuminate certain aspects of the historical field and the merits of each position vis-à-vis the others are relative not absolute.

With these cautions in mind it becomes apparent that in

the discussion in this chapter I have emphasized the differences between Marxist historical writing and that of Foucault. I have done this simply to clarify Foucault's position and also because this chapter remains at the general level of theoretical formation. In the chapters that follow the issues become more specific, the histories of prisons and sexuality. In these contexts also the merits of the positions of Foucault and Marx are subject to relative not absolute judgements.

NOTES

1. A major exception is the work of Dominick La Capra, especially in *History and Criticism* (Ithaca: Cornell University Press, forthcoming).
2. James Henretta, 'Social History as Lived and Written', *American Historical Review*, No. 84 (December, 1979), p. 1299.
3. Allan Megill, 'Foucault, Structuralism, and the Ends of History', *Journal of Modern History*, No. 51 (September, 1979), p. 451–503.
4. Michel Foucault, *The Archeology of Knowledge*, trans. A. M. Sheridan-Smith (New York: Pantheon, 1972), p. 144.
5. Foucault, *Archeology of Knowledge*, p. 12.
6. Michel Foucault, *Discipline and Punish*, trans. A. Sheridan (New York: Pantheon, 1977).
7. Michel Foucault, *The History of Sexuality*, Vol. 1, *An Introduction*, trans. Robert Hurley (New York: Pantheon, 1978).
8. For an excellent supplement to Foucault's *History of Sexuality* on the role of psychoanalysis, see Jacques Donzelot, *The Policing of Families*, trans. Robert Hurley (New York: Pantheon, 1979).
9. Foucault, *Discipline and Punish*, p. 298.
10. The literature of Freudo-Marxism is quite extensive, from Erich Fromm and Wilhelm Reich to Herbert Marcuse, Reimut Reiche, and Michael Schneider. For a critique of this literature, see Mark Poster, *Critical Theory of the Family* (New York: Continuum, 1978), ch. 2.
11. See the important interview, 'Truth and Power', in Michel Foucault, *Power/Knowledge: Selected Interviews and Other Writings,*

1972–1977, ed. Colin Gordon (New York: Pantheon, 1980), pp. 109–33. This piece also appears in 'Michel Foucault: Power, Truth, Strategy', *Working Papers* (1979), pp. 29–48.

12. 'Truth and Power', *Working Papers*, p. 36.

13. For a comparison of Foucault and Althusser on this issue, see P. L. Brown, 'Epistemology and Method: Althusser, Foucault, Derrida', *Cultural Hermeneutics*, No. 3 (August, 1975), p. 147–63. For an excellent, but to my mind finally unconvincing, Marxist critique of Foucault, see Peter Dews. 'The *Nouvelle Philosophie* and Foucault', *Economy and Society* 8 (May, 1979), pp. 127–71. See also Barry Smart, *Foucault, Marxism and Critique* (London: Routledge and Kegan Paul, 1983).

14. For a fine comparison of Habermas and Foucault, see David Hoy, 'Taking History Seriously: Foucault, Gadamer, Habermas', *Union Seminary Quarterly Review*, 34 (Winter, 1979), pp. 85–95.

15. The closest Foucault comes to structuralism is in *Madness and Civilization*, where he defines his project in terms that look very much like those of the structuralists (*Madness and Civilization*, trans. Richard Howard (New York: Vintage, 1965), p. xii. In other works, however, Foucault goes out of his way to insist that he is not one of them. See, for example, 'History, Discourse, and Discontinuity', *Salmagundi*, No. 20 (Summer–Fall, 1972), p. 235n and *Archeology of Knowledge*, p. 11.

16. Foucault, *Archeology of Knowledge*, p. 55.

17. See, for example, Raymond Williams, 'Base and Superstructure', *New Left Review*, No. 82 (November–December, 1973), pp. 3–16.

18. Foucault, 'History, Discourse, Discontinuity', p. 226, where he states: 'Now, I am a pluralist.'

19. Ibid., p. 240.

20. Foucault, *Archeology of Knowledge*, pp. 206–7.

21. Foucault, 'Nietzsche, Genealogy, History', trans. Donald Bouchard and Sherry Simon, in Donald Bouchard (ed.), *Language, Counter-Memory, Practice* (Ithaca: Cornell University Press, 1977), p. 154. Also of interest are Jacques Derrida, *Spurs: Nietzsche's Styles*, trans. Barbara Harlow (Chicago: Chicago University Press, 1979) and Gilles Deleuze, *Nietzsche et la philosophie* (Paris: PUP, 1967). See also the definition given in *Power/Knowledge*, p. 83. For

Foucault's presentism, see Michael Roth, 'Foucault's History of the Present', *History and Theory*, No. 20 (1981), pp. 32–46. Also of interest is the special issue on Foucault of *Humanities in Society*, No. 3 (Winter, 1980), with contributions by Michael Sprinker, Paul Bové, Karlis Racevskis, and Jonathan Arac.

4

Prisons and Surveillance

Discipline and Punish (1975) offers the best example of Foucault's alternative to Marx's historical materialism. In methodology, conceptual development and content, Foucault's book presents a version of critical theory in which the mode of production is not the totalizing center of history. To escape from the confines of Marx's materialism, Foucault turns to Nietzsche and adapts to his own ends the concept of genealogy. As he said in 1976, 'Nowadays I prefer to remain silent about Nietzsche ... If I wanted to be pretentious, I would use 'the genealogy of morals' as the general title of what I am doing.'[1] The new strategy of critique rejects the Hegelian evolutionist model in which one mode of production flows dialectically out of another in favor of a Nietzschean tactic of critique through the presentation of difference.

The methodology of *Discipline and Punish* resounds with dissonance to the ears of Marxists and liberals. Causes and connections are not central concerns for Foucault. The texture of his history of prisons is choppy, disconnected, even arbitrary. But there is a reason for this peculiar approach. Foucault takes his topic, prison systems, and in Nietzschean fashion goes back in time until he finds a point where the prevailing penal practice looks to modern eyes ridiculous, without sense, irrational. The degree of intellectual discomfort is a measure of the difference of that system from our own. Foucault locates such a prison system in the eighteenth century as exemplified in the punishment of the regicide Damiens. The details of Damien's torture colorfully display a world of punishment that is genuinely foreign to our own.

The next analytic step is crucial to the success of the genealogical method. The torture of Damiens must be reconstructed in such a way that the logic of the pre-modern prison system is recaptured. Instead of condemning the barbarism of pre-modern society, its inhumanity, injustice and irrationality, Foucault will present the difference of the pre-modern system by demonstrating that, on its own terms, it makes sense and is coherent. The reason for doing so, let it be noted, is not to present a revised picture of the past, nostalgically to glorify the charms of torture, but to underline the transitory character of the present system and therefore to remove the pretense of legitimacy that it holds by dint of a naive, rationalist contrast with the past. The genealogy of prisons reveals that the modern system is first, finite and second, without exclusive rights to rationality. Since the torture of Damiens is part of a coherent prison system, the modern one is not the only one possible.

By proving the historicity of the modern penal institution Foucault, I maintain, is at one with historical materialism. After all, Marx contended that the purpose of revolutionary criticism was to reveal the historicity of institutions that the dominant ideology pretended were eternal. The first step of the critique was to show that the laws of capitalism were not universally necessary but historically specific. But, if Foucault is Marxist at one point in his methodology, he is anything but Marxist at another. The critical force of Foucault's genealogy derives not, as with Marx, from the demonstration of contradiction within the modern system and therefore of its inevitable collapse at some point in the future, but simply in the difference between the pre-modern and modern structures. There is no hint of dialectical necessity in Foucault's pages, no suggestion that the modern system is less than rational and therefore imperfect. Progressive evolutionism is absent from his account. Instead, the critique relies on the pure demonstration of difference. In short, the appeal to reason, the promise of a more rational world, that is implicit in Marx is lacking in Foucault.

Discipline and Punish begins with a detailed, stomach-turning account of a punishment in the style of the Old Regime:

> On 2 March 1757 Damiens the regicide was condemned 'to make the *amende honorable* before the main door of the Church of Paris,' where he was to be 'taken and conveyed in a cart, wearing nothing but a shirt, holding a torch of burning wax weighing two pounds'; then, 'in the said cart, to the Place de Grève, where, on a scaffold that will be erected there, the flesh will be torn from his breasts, arms, thighs and calves with red-hot pincers, his right hand, holding the knife with which he commited the said pari-cide, burnt with sulphur, and, on those places where the flesh will be torn away, poured molten lead, boiling oil, burning resin, wax and sulphur melted together and then his body drawn and quartered by four horses and his limbs and body consumed by fire, reduced to ashes and his ashes thrown to the winds.'[2]

Such activity was then and remains to this day the nemesis of enlightened reformers and liberals. Damiens' travail was considered by them simply monstrous, beyond nature. What they did not see, or refused to see, was that torture was not an act of gratuitous cruelty in the manner of the isolated murderers and rapists of today, but an orderly social ritual, consciously designed to produce specific effects on the criminal, the offended party and society at large. Damiens' torture was public because it was intended to restore the power of the monarchy, a ritual enactment of the king's power before the world. It marked the flesh of the criminal as a symbolic restoration of the material wrongs he had accomplished. It occurred after a judicial procedure which attempted to arrive at the truth in secret sessions during which a combination of torture and questioning was employed. The prevailing view was that any accused person was not simply guilty or innocent, but subject to gradations of guilt. Once a shred of guilt was proved, torture was a permissible means to get at the rest of the truth. After all, Old Regime logic ran, the guilty party should suffer some punishment. In this way, Foucault argues, the system of punishment of the Old Regime was not pure barbarism, but a 'regulated practice'. It was designed to produce terror in the hearts of the public that witnessed the torture and thereby to reaffirm the power of the ruling class.

The analysis of the torture serves to highlight the difference between pre-modern and modern systems of punishment. Like Nietzsche's description of the ethics of the Vikings who plundered, raped and murdered at whim and with no sense of guilt, Foucault's depiction of Damiens' sufferings convinces one that a system of punishment other than our own is possible. This strategy serves to define and limit the temporal scope of the modern system. It was begun after the old system was overthrown and it has characteristics that are not those of the past. The remarkable achievement of Foucault's Nietzschean discourse is that it captures the past without justifying the present, as liberals do, or anticipating an evolutionary, utopian future, the way Marxists do. The display of the difference of the past avoids the danger of dismissing it (as barbarism) and thereby legitimating the present, in the manner of liberals, as a superior and unsurpassable world. As for Marxists, they take the punishment system of the Old Regime and 'explain' it by reference to the mode of production. The function and limits of this type of explanation will be discussed below. But for now it can be said that Marxist accounts are similar to liberals' in that they implicitly condemn eighteenth-century practices and assume that the future rational world of communism will automatically abolish the embarrassing infantilisms of earlier ages. Both liberals and Marxists advocate reason in place of past practices, legitimating their own positions without exploring the genealogical radicalism of what they reject.

After the presentation of difference in the torture of Damiens, Foucault continues his genealogy of prison systems with an account of proposals for reform. The *philosophes* of the Enlightenment reacted vehemently against the punishment system of the Old Regime. Thinkers like Cesare Beccaria in *On Crimes and Punishments* (1764) wished to humanize punishment by eliminating torture, reducing the power of the monarch and above all regularizing the impact of the judicial system. Believing in the force of reason, the reformers wished to shift the locus of punishment from the body to the mind, to present to criminals the certain prospect that their acts would cause more pain than pleasure so that, as rational beings, they would avoid committing illegalities in the first place. Yet the plans of the philosophes were not to become the basis for the new system of punishment that emerged in the nineteenth century. The centerpiece of that system — the prison — was, Foucault notes, 'explicitly criticized by many reformers. Because it is incapable of corresponding to the specificity of crimes. Because it has no effect on the public. Because it is useless, even harmful, to society.'[3] In effect, the modern system of punishment based on incarceration is separated, for the genealogist, from the system of torture by a sharp discontinuity.

The gap between the old and the new serves to underscore in yet another way the principle of difference at the heart of Foucault's historiography. By allowing the discontinuity to remain unexplained, he violates the assumptions of both liberal and Marxist methods. The role of cause or explanation is severely reduced in the post-structuralist text, since it leads to evolutionist conclusions and works against the purposes of the genealogy of difference. Let us be clear about this point. Foucault does attempt to explain certain historical phenomena and he does provide evolutionary histories at certain points in his text. There is no question of ruling out entirely the role of cause, explanation, evolution. It is only that if these methodological strategies predominate in the historical text, the critical function of difference will be lost. Foucault is not proposing a new metaphysics of history in which one age is ontologically separate from the others. Rather he attempts to extract from the complexity of the past certain lines of struggle because, he thinks, they can have an impact on the way we think about the structures of domination in the present.

Although the ideas of the eighteenth century reformers did not materialize into a new system of punishment, those of Jeremy Bentham were more successful. In fact, Bentham's *Panopticon* was the leading antecedent of the new technology of power than was instituted in the nineteenth century prison. There are three features of Foucault's understanding of the prison system that are important for critical theory. First, the specific features of the prison as Foucault sees it are significant to the comprehension of the new role of information systems in advanced capitalism. Second, the manner in which Foucault explores the prison system as a structure of domination suggests a detotalized version of critical theory. Third, Foucault's method of introducing the conceptual basis of his genealogy (for example, the concept of technology of power) leaves unresolved certain epistemological questions for critical theory.

The nineteenth-century system of punishment bore little resemblance to that of the Old Regime. Incarceration, a minor feature of the eighteenth-century penal system, quickly became the norm in the nineteenth century. Secret judicial proceedings were exchanged for public trials. Public tortures gave way to secret or hidden terms of imprisonment. The contrasts between the two systems are elaborated in detail by Foucault. But attention to the differences should not obscure the unique features of the prison. A total institution, as sociologists would say, was established in which even the minutest details of the everyday life of the inmate were enunciated in rules. Some of the features of the prison regimen were derived from earlier practices. The careful control of the temporal and spatial location of the bodies of the inmates was taken from old military practices. In this specific case Foucault acknowledges an evolutionary connection across discontinuous phenomena. What is to Foucault the astonishing new feature of the prison system, however, is the method by which the prison authorities sought to control the minds of the prison population. Bentham advocated that the prisoners be housed in a rectangular structure that surrounded a courtyard, in the middle of which was a tower containing a guard. The building was arranged so that the guard was able to see into each cell without himself being seen by the prisoners. Hence the term Panopticon (all-seeing). The ingenious purpose served by this arrangement was that the prisoner would be conscious of being under continual surveillance. The guard, a representative of society's authority, became a kind of God-surrogate who could observe the prisoner at will, monitor behavioral abberations or improvements and mete out rewards and punishments accordingly. Foucault does not draw attention to the likeness of the Panopticon and the Christian God's infinite knowledge. Nor does he observe the similarity of the Panopticon with Freud's notion of the super-ego as an internal monitor of unconscious wishes. An even closer parallel that goes unnoticed by Foucault is that between the Panopticon and the computer monitoring of individuals in advanced capitalism, a point I shall return to shortly.

Before turning to the latter comparison, I want to emphasize certain features of the Panopticon. Foucault sees the Panopticon as a technique for controlling large numbers of people in a particular institution, or, what he calls, discipline, as in the following description of a quarantine during an epidemic:

> This enclosed, segmented space, observed at every point, in which
> the individuals are inserted in a fixed place, in which the slightest
> movements are supervised, in which all events are recorded, in
> which an uninterrupted work of writing links the centre and
> periphery, in which power is exercised without division, according
> to a continuous hierarchical figure, in which each individual is
> constantly located, examined and distributed among the living
> beings, the sick and the dead – all this constituted a compact
> model of the disciplinary method.[4]

Applying the methods of discipline to the prison through the
architecture of the Panopticon transforms simple incarceration into a diabolical means of punishment. The problem
faced by prison administrators of controlling masses of
people led them to turn to the solution of the Panopticon
and thereby changed the effects of incarceration from simple
removal from society to total power over the inmate. In
Foucault's words, 'Hence the major effect of the Panoptican:
to induce in the inmate a state of conscious and permanent
visibility that assures the automatic functioning of power.'[5]
From the Enlightenment desire to abolish torture we have
moved to a new type of punishment, unanticipated by the
reformers of the eighteenth century, which in effect institutes
a new system of domination. The effect of the Panopticon is
not to reform prisoners: we know that recidivism rates have
always been high. Instead it introduces a method of normalizing individuals that can be applied to other situations.
As Foucault writes, 'All that is needed, then is to place a
supervisor in a central tower and to shut up in each cell a
madman, a patient, a condemned man, a worker or a school-
boy.[6] Capitalist society thus has available a means of control,
a 'technology of power' that can be deployed at many
locations.

When the Panopticon was introduced in the early nineteenth century the bureaucracy and the computer had not yet been invented. Foucault does not mention that they both foster the principles of disciplinary control. Indeed they expand its scope to a new level. With the mechanisms of information processing (the bureaucracy using people; the computer using machines), the ability to monitor behavior is extended considerably. The techniques of discipline no longer need rely on methods of regulating bodies in space as Foucault thinks. In the electronic age, spatial limitations are bypassed as restraints on the controlling hierarchies. All that is needed are traces of behavior; credit card activity, traffic tickets, telephone bills, loan applications, welfare files, fingerprints, income transactions, library records, and so forth. On the basis of these traces, a computer can gather information that yields a surprisingly full picture of an individual's life. As a consequence, Panopticon monitoring extends not simply to massed groups but to the isolated individual. The normalized individual is not only the one at work, in an asylum, in jail, in school, in the military, as Foucault observes, but also the individual in his or her home, at play, in all the mundane activities of everyday life.[7]

If the scope of Foucault's analysis of the prison system is extended by an understanding of the impact of information systems in advanced capitalism, the theoretical problems his position encounters are only increased. Foucault wants to argue that he is simply tracing the genealogy of the prison system, a specific phenomenon that is best left untotalized. He himself is tempted by the totalizing impulse at several points in his text, most notably when he writes:

> ... the activity of judging has increased precisely to the extent that the normalizing power has spread. Borne along by the omnipresence of the mechanisms of discipline, basing itself on all the carceral apparatuses, it has become one of the major functions of our society. The judges of normality are present everywhere. We are in the society of the teacher-judge, the doctor-judge, the

educator-judge, the 'social worker'-judge; it is on them that the
universal reign of the normative is based.[8]

The impression given by this passage is that the mode of
normalization has replaced the mode of production as the
basis of a new totalization with a new set of structures of
domination. Yet Foucault wishes to argue the opposite,
Nietzschean standpoint: that 'technologies of power' are
multiple and not reducible to each other; that critical theory
is best served by detotalized analyses which restrict themselves
to particular clusters of dominating practices; that epistemologically there is no basis for any theorist to assert a totalizing
view since we are each limited by our situated perspectives.
Most significantly Foucault agrees with the Nietzschean
viewpoint that power is creative, not repressive; that technologies of power emerge at multiple points in social space
and are not located in the state, as liberals and Marxists think.
A disservice is done to critical theory when the distinct but
interrelated technologies of power endured by women, racial
minorities, gays, prisoners, inmates of asylums and workers
are reduced, even with the caution of mediations, to the
monothithic 'mode of production'.

Marxists who have written about the history of prisons
have missed the unique features of the Panopticon for precisely these reasons. Reducing systems of punishment to the
class structure, they have been unable to discern the technology of power of the prison system. The classic work of
Georg Rusche and Otto Kirchheimer (an associate of the
Frankfurt School), *Punishment and Social Structure*, reveals
the limitations of Marxist theory. They begin their analysis
in typical Marxist fashion by rejecting illusory ideological
formations in favor of what they regard as real social relationships. Their aim is ' . . . to strip from the social institution
of punishment its ideological veils and justice appearance and
to describe it in its real realtionships'.[9] Their conclusion consists of the inevitable Marxist pronouncement: 'specific

forms of punishment correspond to a given stage of economic development.'[10] The history of prisons provides nothing more than an epiphenomenon to the history of the mode of production.

Rusche and Kirchheimer explain various aspects of the pre-modern system of punishment in strictly reductionist terms. In the late middle ages, for example, 'The poorer the masses became the harsher the punishments in order to deter them from crime.'[11] These same economic factors account for 'the death penalty and serious multilation'.[12] With respect to the galley as a form of punishment, their argument is consistent: 'What is significant in the development of the galley as a method of punishment is the fact that economic considerations alone were involved, not penal.'[13] They conclude that the substitution of galley service for the death penalty was motivated not by humanitarianism but by economics.[14] It is clear that the Marxist approach as employed by Rusche and Kirchheimer makes no effort to make intelligible the pre-modern system of punishment as a unique technology of power.

When they turn to the prison system their strategy remains the same. 'Of all the forces which were responsible for the new emphasis upon imprisonment as a punishment, the most important was the profit motive, both in the narrower sense of making the establishment pay and in the wider sense of making the whole penal system a part of the state's mercantilist program.'[15] The object of knowledge made intelligible by the Marxist perspective consistently ignores all forms of domination that are not reducible to the mode of production. Bentham's *Panopticon* and the prisons that installed its principles in their architecture during the nineteenth century are not even mentioned. Finally, and perhaps most importantly, Rusche and Kirchheimer betray the close connection of Marxism to liberalism. They pay homage to the advance of the human sciences, as any good liberal would, but they have an explanation for the failure of criminology to lead to the solution of the question of crime.

> There is a paradox in the fact that the progress of human know-
> ledge has made the problem of penal treatment more comprehen-
> sible and more soluble than ever while the question of a funda-
> mental revision in the policy of punishment seems to be further
> away today that ever before because of its functional dependence
> on a given social order (i.e. capitalism).[16]

In this passage Rusche and Kirchheimer execute the Marxist
tactic of unmasking liberal ideology: valid knowledge does
not lead to social progress because of the interference of the
capitalist mode of production. What is revealing is that they
take at face value the purpose of the prison system: i.e. to
solve the question of crime. Foucault takes a different
approach, as we have seen, one that allows him to reveal a
different sort of social maneuver. He considers the prison
system not in terms of solving the problem of crime, but as
instituting a system of power that is transferable to other
social institutions and has its effect as a new structure of
domination.

The point of this discussion is not to dismiss the Marxist
case, only to indicate its limitations. Foucault in fact is
careful to praise Rusche and Kirchheimer. He also notes
connections between the history of prisons and the mode
of production wherever he finds them. He relates 'the formation of disciplinary society' with 'a number of broad historical
processes', among them the development of capitalism.[17] An
important element in the conjuncture of the birth of prisons,
he states, 'was the growth in the apparatus of production,
which was becoming more and more extended and complex;
it was also becoming more costly and its profitability had to
be increased. The development of the disciplinary methods
corresponded to these two processes, or rather, no doubt,
to the new need to adjust their correlation.[18] More concretely,
Foucault relates the increase in new forms of crime (illegali-

ties, he calls them) to the emerging capitalist economy. One of the driving motives behind the reformers' quest for greater regularity of punishment than was offered by the Old Regimes' system of torture was the rapid increase in new types of theft, of crimes against property. Foucault repeats Marx's argument in 'The Case of the Wood Theft Laws': capitalism transformed the traditional rights of the poor into crimes against property. Traditional theft of small game, for example, 'while resented by the bourgeoisie where the ownership of land was concerned, was intolerable in commercial and industrial ownership: the development of ports, the appearance of great warehouses in which merchandise was stored, the organization of huge workshops . . . also necessitated a severe repression of illegality.'[19] Evidently, Foucault is not hostile to Marxist interpretive strategies. In fact, he admits that,

> It is impossible at the present time to write history without using a whole range of concepts directly or indirectly linked to Marx's thought and situating oneself within a horizon of thought which has been defined and described by Marx. One might even wonder what difference there could ultimately be between being a historian and being a Marxist.[20]

Nevertheless Foucault finds Marxism insufficient. The conceptual arsenal of Marxism does not permit one to go beyond the mode of production to make intelligible the forms of domination that emerge at other points in social space and, in addition, to regard these forms of domination as conceptually distinct from the relations of production. For Marxists, prisoners and criminals are a marginal group. Analysis of their experience fails to reveal significant repressive apparatuses, nor does it make intelligible sources of radicality that contribute to the overthrow of the social order. For Foucault, on the contrary, with his detotalized assumptions, systems of power and domination exist at multiple locations, each one being unique, and, as in the case of the Panopticon, some revealing at least as much about the repressive nature of modern society as the analysis of capitalist domination.

Since the appearance of *Discipline and Punish* Marxist historians of the prison have wrestled with the challenge Foucault's book presents to their theoretical assumptions. At least in two important cases, Michael Ignatieff's *A Just Measure of Pain* (1978) and Patricia O'Brien's *The Promise of Punishment* (1982), the test has been met in most satisfactory ways. Both Ignatieff and O'Brien acknowledge the value of *Discipline and Punish* and manage to integrate its advances into more traditionally Marxist approaches. A detotalized Marxist historiography may thus be compatible with Foucault's interpretive strategy.

Ignatieff explicitly takes *Discipline and Punish* as his point of departure. Given the features of the Panoptical penitentiary as Foucault analyses them, Ignatieff attempts to explain how at the ideological level the new system of punishment could be a progressive step. *A Just Measure of Pain*, he proposes,

> . . . tries to establish why it came to be considered just, reasonable, and humane to immure prisoners in solitary cells, clothe them in uniforms, regiment their day to the cadence of the clock, and 'improve' their minds with dosages of scripture and hard labor. Between 1770 and 1840 this form of carceral discipline 'directed at the mind' replaced a cluster of punishments 'directed at the body – whipping, branding, the stocks, and public hanging.[21]

Ignatieff accepts Foucault's critique of the liberal view of incarceration and seeks to push liberal ideology as far as he can so that an opening can be breached for a Marxist critique of it.

As a consequence of Foucault's study of prisons, the Marxist historian can no longer be satisfied with explaining directly the emergence of the penitentiary by the needs of the capitalist mode or production. At least one more step is now required: the logic of domination within the prison must be taken into account. The liberal position that prisons were a humane improvement over torture is not treated, as it was in Rusche and Kirchheimer, as a ruse of Capital whose interests were the 'underlying cause' of the new method of punishment. Instead, the Marxist historian may now confront the liberal position on its own grounds, questioning explicitly the moral advance of the bourgeois system of treating criminals.

Ignatieff frames his work in this more subtle Marxist strategy. His subtitle is 'The Penitentiary in the Industrial Revolution', a phrase that asserts the Marxist priority of the mode of production. But the specific issue he addresses is the ideological and political dimension of punishment: 'a study of prison discipline', he argues, 'necessarily becomes a study . . . of the moral boundaries of social authority in a society undergoing capitalist transformation.'[22] Rather than simply looking at the machinations of the capitalist class, Ignatieff devotes the bulk of his study to the intellectual justifications of the prison system, especially as the political and cultural elite gradually becomes aware of its limitations. As the disturbing details of prison life intruded into public consciousness in nineteenth-century England (Ignatieff's field of research), the bastions of order were hardpressed to sustain their rosy image of the humanity of incarceration. And yet they did just that.

Ignatieff concludes therefore that the continued legitimacy afforded the prison system derived not from its inherently humane qualities, but from the imperatives of domination in bourgeois society. He concludes, as Foucault did, that the Panopticon instituted a technology of power that was its own political justification, belying its humanitarian claims:

The persistent support for the penitentiary is inexplicable so long

as we assume that its appeal rested on its functional capacity to
control crime. Instead, its support rested on a larger social need.
It had appeal because the reformers succeeded in presenting it
as a response, not merely to crime, but to the whole social crisis
of a period, and as part of a larger strategy of political, social, and
legal reform designed to reestablish order on a new foundation . . .
it was seen as an element of a larger vision of order that by the
1840s commanded the reflexive assent of the propertied and
powerful.[23]

The Marxist history of prisons thus confronts the political
issue of a structure of domination not reducible to the mode
of production.

O'Brien's history of prisons, in this case those of nineteenth-century France, responds to *Discipline and Punish*
in a manner different from Ignatieff. *The Promise of Punishment* is framed as a social history, history 'from the bottom
up'. As such it derives from E. P. Thompson's classic text,
The Making of the English Working Class (1963). Thompson
there revises the standard Marxist historical strategy by
emphasizing the creative response of the oppressed to their
conditions of life. The subjective side of the dialectic is re-
invigorated, as the issue for Thompson is not the weight of
capitalist structures on the proletariat but their resistance to
them. The model Thompson provides has served well a new
generation of Marxist social historians who are unhappy with
merely enumerating the burdens suffered by the working
class.[24]

O'Brien's book is a credit to the tradition established by
Thompson. With a humanity that avoids sentimentality, she
analyses in depth the group of souls who inhabited the peni-
tentiaries of France. She presents composite portraits of the
male, female and child prisoner, noting how their features
change in the course of the nineteenth century. Unlike
Foucault's account of the Panopticon, in which the impression is given that all prisoners were dealt with in the same

fashion, O'Brien reveals how each category of prisoner presented unique problems for the penitentiary system and was handled in quite different ways. The single cell system, the standard for the adult male prisoner, was thought by many to be unsuitable for the female convict whose constitution was considered weaker than the male's and whose moral character was imagined to be more pliant. Child prisoners were in general not subject to the Panopticon at all, but secluded in rural work farms. Children were not isolated in cells but banded into living groups called 'families'. For the worst offenders the penitentiary was likewise unsuitable; they were shipped out to the infamous penal colonies. Thus the penitentiary was not at all a uniform system applied equally to all criminals. What is more, the nature of the criminal group required alterations in the system of punishment. In other words, the characteristics of the subjects led to variations in the technology of power employed. Foucault, it will be recalled, avoided reference to the subjects in his analysis. O'Brien's account of the variety of treatment of prisoners suggests that the subjects should indeed be brought into the historical drama. If this is not done the historian cannot describe or explain the limitations of the dissemination of the disciplinary system of punishment.

Not only did the objective traits of the prison population affect the nature and extent of the Panopticon model, but so too did the response of that group to their punishments. The prisoners, in O'Brien's account, were not an inert mass passively accepting the dictates of the new mode of domination. Rather they responded to the administration of their lives by resisting in different ways the impositions placed upon them. They rioted, they refused to participate in the routines established for them, they developed their own language, they tattooed their bodies, they engaged in illicit forms of sexuality – in short they created a prisoner subculture. This subculture established statuses, hierarchies and norms and was spread from prison to prison by the recidivists. The guards and prison authorities were helpless in eradicating this culture, even when, as in the case of homosexual practices, they regarded the behavior as noxious. O'Brien demonstrates for French prisoners what we know to be the case from studies of Nazi extermination camps: human beings have the capacity to resist even the most extreme forms of authority and the authorities inevitably accept most aspects of the subjugated group's culture because administration of the institution would collapse without it. The impression left by *Discipline and Punish* of the passivity of prisoners faced with Panoptical regimentation must be corrected. Of course, Foucault does not argue that the prisoners obeyed the guards. He says very little about the response of the prisoners to the new system of authority, since he is only concerned with the characteristics of the new technology of power. Nevertheless, O'Brien's construction of the culture of the prisoners as an active creation of resistance serves as a valuable corrective to Foucault's work.

There are still other features of *The Promise of Punishment* that illuminate the history of prisons. In the course of the nineteenth century French prisons became factories: they produced commodities for the market. Prison labor was organized and supervised most often by businessmen who significantly were placed in charge of the surveillance and discipline of the inmates. The administration of the Panopticon was not solely the work of the guards, but was shared by capitalists. If the new technology of power spread to the capitalist mode of production, or indeed was partly influenced by it, one need look no further than this group of entrepeneurs for the link between prison and factory. Moreover, the work of the prisoners brought them into conflict with the working class. In some instances prison production presented a challenge to the proletariat; the prisoners were a cheap source of labor in competition with the 'free' labor market. In all of these ways O'Brien adds a new dimension to our understanding of the relation between capitalism and the penitentiary. In contrast to Rusche and Kirchheimer, Foucault is right to assert that the capitalist mode of production did not 'determine' the origins and nature of the prison system. But the actual relationship between the two institutions is more complicated than that. The prison served as a training ground for capitalists in the new technology of power and it spawned a 'class struggle' pitting inmates against the proletariat, developments that fit neatly into neither the traditional Marxist nor Foucault's model.

O'Brien concludes her social history of the prison from the bottom up with a revised image of the prisoner class. In the early nineteenth century prisoners were seen by the elites as a segment of the working class. They were a group born to and created by conditions of poverty. The couplet 'laboring classes, dangerous classes' summed up the prevalent attitude toward criminals. By the end of the century the criminal 'element' was no longer associated with the proletariat. The Panopticon had produced 'the hardened criminal', a new social type whose recidivism could be explained not as a consequence of poverty but as a result of life in the penitentiary itself. The emerging human science of criminology and associated disciplines produced 'knowledge' about the criminal class that thwarted attempts to identify it solely with the proletariat. Specific traits of heredity and personality were the new determinants of social disorder. It is a fascinating story: the new technology of power is set into place; its subjects resist; recidivism emerges as an index of the failure of liberalism; a human science is born which 'explains' the failure in a way that deflects blame from the bourgeoisie and relocates it in the remote realms of genetics and psychology, indirectly legitimizing the Panopticon.

The Promise of Punishment adds immeasurably to the accomplishment of *Discipline and Punish*. In that way it only reinforces the argument against totalizing historical theory. At the same time it eloquently speaks for the combination of Marxist and Foucauldian perspectives. And yet

the question of the status of the subject in Foucault's discourse and more generally a theory of resistance remains
open. Foucault's chief argument remains intact: the disciplinary technology of power is made intelligible only by
constituting the historical field outside the perspectives of
the subject. And yet, thus constituted the object of history
(discourse/practice) is inadequate in accounting for resistance.

The achievement of *Discipline and Punish* goes beyond its
value for a history of prisons in the nineteenth century. It
raises in addition questions about a form of domination in
the twentieth century and it does so in two distinct ways.
First, Foucault's text analyses the disciplinary technology
of power in relation to surveillance. As I indicated above,
new technologies concerned with electronic information
extend the reach of surveillance far beyond its nineteenth-
century limits. The vast ability of the established authorities
to gather information about individuals or groups places in
question or even eliminates the distinction between the public
and the private. At this time it is not possible to estimate the
impact on the population of this surveillance capability.

There is another side to the question of surveillance, one
that is more indirect than the monitoring of individuals.
Discipline and Punish astutely draws a connection between
surveillance and normalization. The prison was designed
to rehabilitate criminals, to re-orient their minds and behavior in a manner closer to that of the non-criminal, normal
population. Crime is abnormal. The guards are trained to be
alert to deviations from the norms of the pententiary routines.
Implicit in surveillance systems is the criterion of the norm.
Surveillance selects out for examination those items that are
different from the norm. A black man walking at night in a
white suburban neighborhood is suspect. Loud laughter or
dance-like movements in an exclusive department store are
signs that alert the security system. Normalization is dissem-
inated throughout daily life and secured through surveillance
monitoring.

Still another level removed from the surveillance of prisoners pertains to surveillance through the electronic communications media. These information systems rely upon normalizing criteria in constituting their audiences. The communications media speak to the population, but they do so without the feedback information of two-way conversations. They are constrained to organize their emissions in such a manner that the receiver can accept them. The receiver must be a general receiver, without too many individualized traits, not a real person but a fictionalized norm of a person. By the same token, the receiver of the message must transform him or herself into the norm in order to comprehend the message as it was intended. The receiver must become the norm. One can resist, at least for a while. A literary critic watching a TV show can maintain a distance and take note of grammatical mistakes, vulgar characterization, and so forth. A black person can be aware that the values implicit in the show are racist. A recent immigrant can recognize the alien mores of a different culture in network dramas. Yet inevitably each one will gradually accept the norms displayed on the screen and come to regard them as the real norms. It is fair to say that the result of the receiver's self-transformation is a kind of surveillance practiced continuously in advanced industrial society. The mode of information enormously extends the reach of normalizing surveillance, constituting new modes of domination that have yet to be studied.

The second way that Foucault's text raises questions about the mode of domination in the twentieth century concerns the concept of discourse and the treatment of language more generally. Against the assertion that *Discipline and Punish* should be interpreted as a history of prisons Foucault counters that it must be evaluated in relation to a history of reason:

What is at stake in the 'birth of the prison'? French society in a given period? No. Delinquency in the 18th and 19th centuries? No. Prisons in France between 1760 and 1840? Not even that . . .

In short it is a question of a chapter in the history of 'punitive reason'.[25]

Foucault's topic is thus discourse, discourse of a certain type.

As we have seen, in the case of prisons Foucault relates the discourses of certain human sciences to the practices instituted in the penitentiary. The couplet discourse/ practice is intended to bypass the traditional separation between attitudes and behavior, language and action in the historical field. Critical social theory has not looked favorably on positions rooted in theories of language, such as Foucault's concept of discourse. In *The German Ideology* Marx relegated language to a minor place in social theory.

> From the start the 'spirit' bears the curse of being 'burdened' with matter which makes its appearance in the form of agitated layers of air, sounds, in short, in the form of language. Language is as old as consciousness. It *is* practical consciousness which exists also for other men and hence exists for me personally as well. Language, like consciousness, only arises [*entsteht*] from the need and necessity of relationships with other men.[26]

The 'need and necessity of relationships with other men' becomes the central concern of historical materialism. Language tends to be analysed in the form of ideology, as obscuring and mystifying human relationships. Workers act; the bourgeoisie justifies the structure of action through language.

Foucault's concept of discourse must be viewed in this light if its advantages are to be grasped. First, Foucault rejected the split between knowledge and power, discourse and practice. Since, as Nietzsche had shown, knowledge was a form of power and since power created and shaped practice rather than limited it, discourse was deeply implicated in the critique of domination. This strategy required that discourse be analyzed not as a form of consciousness, not as an expression of the subject, but as a form of positivity. The rejection of the subjectivity of discourse led Foucault in *The Archeology of Knowledge* to elaborate a new set of categories that would allow discourse to stand on its own as a form of power.

> I shall abandon any attempt . . . to see discourse as a phenomenon of expression – the verbal translation of a previously established synthesis; instead, I shall look for a field of regularity for various positions of subjectivity. Thus conceived, discourse is not the majestically unfolding manifestation of a thinking, knowing, speaking subject, but, on the contrary, a totality, in which the dispersion of the subject, and his discontinuity with himself may be determined.[27]

This is a concept of discourse (language) appropriate to a critical theory of the mode of information, one that, properly understood, remains materialist because it points to the analysis of modes of domination in contemporary social space.

Historical materialism is based on the conviction that the object of historical knowledge cannot be ideas, because the ideas that people hold about social existence do not determine their existence. Marx formulated this salutary principle at a time when historical thinking, especially in Germany, was indeed idealist. At that time however, in the mid-nineteenth century, vast social changes were occurring in the organization of political and economic action. A theory grounded in idealism was particularly unsuited to lay bare the structures of these political and economic transformations. But what must become of historical materialism at a time when the structures of linguistic experience are undergoing drastic change – when bureaucracies accumulate extensive files on the population; when visual and aural electronic impulses (TV, telephone, radio, film) constitute significant portions of the communications in everyday life; when commodities are produced through the mediation of computers and sold through the mediation of clusters of meanings generated by advertising teams; when political processes are shaped by mass communication devices; when the digital logic of the computer threatens to extend itself into every corner of the social world; when the human sciences and the natural sciences are integrated into the systems of social control and reproduction? In this context, historical materialism must do more than calculate rates of exploitation and declining profit margins. It must do more than demonstrate the alienated conditions of the act of labor. Indeed, it must take into account these new forms of language; it must develop categories to analyze the patterns of domination and distortion inherent in their contemporary usage, and it must examine the historical stages of their development.

Employing only the traditional categories of Marxism, perhaps adjusted by the traditions of Western Marxism, one would learn how the new systems of language serve the ruling class and are controlled to some degree by them.[28] While that is a valid enterprise, it is not by itself adequate for the analysis of the mode of information. Foucault's recent work is useful precisely on this account. *Discipline and Punish* avoids centering critical theory on a totalizing concept of labor. It grasps structures of domination in their specifity and, while relating different patterns of domination to each other, resists the temptation to reduce one to another. In addition, the book employs a notion of discourse, elaborated further in *The History of Sexuality*, which sanctions the analysis of language yet avoids grounding it in subjectivity. Critical theory thus has an example of an examination of a structure of domination in language that is not rooted in idealist assumptions. For these reasons aspects of Foucault's methodology are valuable for a critical theory of the mode of information. In chapter 6 I shall present the main outlines of the concept of the mode of information. Before doing that I must examine *The History of Sexuality*, paying particular attention to the development by Foucault of the concept of discourse.

NOTES

1. *Power/Knowledge: Selected Interviews and Other Writings, 1972–1977*, ed. Colin Gordon (New York: Pantheon, 1980), p. 53.
2. *Discipline and Punish: The Birth of the Prison*, trans. Alan Sheridan (New York: Pantheon, 1977), p. 3.
3. Ibid., p. 114.
4. Ibid., p. 197.
5. Ibid., p. 201.
6. Ibid., p. 200.
7. I do not mean to adopt the standard attitude toward the spread of computer technology: that is, that it will solve all society's problems and will replace all other forms of technology. An excellent example of an analysis of the introduction of one computer technology is found in Rob Kling, 'Value Conflicts and Social Choice in Electronic Funds Transfer System Developments', *Communications of the ACM*, Vol. 21, No. 8 (August, 1978), pp. 642–57. Kling demonstrates how the values and interests of various social groups are affected by the introduction of a new computer technology. The resulting picture is shaded in greys; different groups are affected differently, some benefit, some do not. Only naive ideologists can make themselves believe in an utopia through computers.
8. *Discipline and Punish*, p. 304.
9. Georg Rusche and Otto Kirchheimer, *Punishment and Social Structure* (New York: Russell and Russell, 1968, original edition 1939), trans. M. Finkelstein, p. 5.
10. Ibid., p. 6.
11. Ibid., p. 18.
12. Ibid., p. 19.
13. Ibid., p. 55.
14. Ibid., p. 57.
15. Ibid., p. 68–9.
16. Ibid., p. 207.
17. *Discipline and Punish*, p. 218.
18. Ibid.
19. Ibid., p. 85.
20. *Power/Knowledge*, p. 53.

21. Micheal Ignatieff, *A Just Measure of Pain: The Penitentiary in the Industrial Revolution, 1750–1850* (New York: Columbia University Press, 1978), p. xiii.
22. Ibid.
23. Ibid., p. 210.
24. Patricia A. O'Brien, *The Promise of Punishment: Prisons in Nineteenth Century France* (Princeton: Princeton University Press, 1982). See also her essay, 'Crime and Punishment as Historical Problem', *Journal of Social History* (1978), pp. 508–20, where she evaluates *Discipline and Punish*.
25. Michelle Perrot (ed.), *L'Impossible Prison: Recherches sur le système pénitentiaire au XIXe siècle* (Paris: Editions du Seuil, 1980), p. 33.
26. Easton and Guddat, eds., *The Writings of the Young Marx on Philosophy and Society* (New York: Anchor, 1967), p. 421.
27. *The Archeology of Knowledge*, p. 55.
28. Herbert Schiller, *Who Knows: Information in the Age of the Fortune 500* (New York: Ablex, 1981).

5

True Discourses on Sexuality

Shortly after the appearance of *Discipline and Punish* Foucault initiated a new project, the study of the history of sexuality. A short prolegomenon to the project was published in 1976, tracing the methodological outlines and general themes of the larger effort. *The History of Sexuality, Volume 1*, therefore, presented no research and contained no finished knowledge, although this did not deter critics from attacking the book as if its hypotheses were really final statements. The book is germane to this study for its development of the concept of discourse/practice and for its clarification of Foucault's antithetical relation to Western Marxists, in this case in the form of Freudo-Marxism.

Since World War I sexuality has become a topic of increasing concern among social theorists. In the 1920s popular culture in Europe and the United States shifted away from the pre-war Victorian ethos of respectability and rushed toward a more uninhibited way of life, one that acknowledged openly the pleasures of the flesh. In the context of the Roaring Twenties, psychoanalysis was taken as a theoretical support for overturning constraints on sexuality. Freud appeared to demonstrate the validity of the new middle-class ethos: restrictions on sexual activity were harmful mentally and physically. Psychoanalytic theory provided an alibi for those who, rejecting Christian and bourgeois asceticism, heralded a great revolution in sexual behavior.

Although isolated figures in the past, such as Charles Fourier in the nineteenth century, had advocated sexual liberation, Wilhelm Reich initiated a trend in the twentieth century which elevated sexuality to a primary place in social thought.[1] Reich gave shape to a mode of thought that has grown in importance since his day. Combining ideas from Marx and Freud, he formulated a theory of sexual revolution that oriented most thinking on the topic. If Marx provided a radical critique of the organization of labor, Reich argued, so Freud invented a radical critique of the organization of love. Work and sex, he contended, needed to be freed from their capitalist and patriarchal prisons. The synthesis of Marx and Freud proposed by Reich was in his eyes a blissful union. Both thinkers were pronounced thoroughly dialectical. In addition, the history of the mode of production and mode of reproduction (or sexuality) were parallel and harmonious. Knowledge about one increased knowledge about the other. Changes in the economy and changes in sexual organization occurred simultaneously and in the same direction.

From Reich's formulation emerged a history of sex that has had great success among radical social theorists. The onset of capitalism, the story goes, marked an increase in the level of sexual repression. When the bourgeoisie took control of the social order, it instituted a regime of sexual denial never before experienced. The authoritarian bourgeois father, devoted obsessively to accumulating capital, hoarded his energies for the marketplace and factory. The preoccupation with saving extended from the realm of work to the realm of the bedroom. Financial economy was matched by spermatic economy. Freud's characterization of contemporary capitalist society as 'the high-water mark of sexual repression' was easily explained by Reich as the direct consequence of the rule of the bourgeoisie.

In the history of sexuality stemming from Reich's Freudo-

Marxism, an assumption had crept into social theory which both Freudians and Marxists might find wanting. Reich had introduced naturalism into the theories. For Reich labor and sexuality could be reduced to bodily needs. Socialism could be understood as an improved dietary regimen, and psycho-analysis was a method of attaining more pleasureful orgasms. Marx and Freud were theorists of health — the former of nutrition, the latter of sex — and social criticism was rooted in the natural needs of the body. Since capitalism failed to provide good food for the working class and patriarchy failed to provide good sex for the working class, these social arrangements required basic transformation.

Recent Freudo-Marxists have not overcome the flaws in Reich's original positions. They have attempted, however, to update the history of sex by accounting for the loosening of sexual restrictions since World War II. Herbert Marcuse, Reimut Reiche, Michael Schneider, and others have offered explanations for the apparent collapse of bourgeois Victorianism. The severe prudishness of nineteenth-century capitalism has been converted into ·the frenetic sensualism of advanced capitalism. In the short space of a century sexual mores have completely altered, or so it seems. Wife swapping; swinging parties; sex therapies; pornographic or erotic films, books, and magazines; varieties of sexual aids; places like Plato's Retreat — these phenomena are evidence, in their wide proliferation, of an intense quest for sexual fulfillment and gratification.

Freudo-Marxists have explained the overnight turnabout in sexual mores in a variety of ways. Marcuse argued that the so-called sexual revolution is not a threat to the established order but only another method this order employs to control the populace.[2] Although traditional repressions have been lifted, a new kind of repression of sexuality — repressive desublimation — has been substituted for the older type. Unable to maintain the asceticism of the past, capitalist society has defused the potential threat posed by demands for sexual liberation by channeling them into acceptable outlets. Emotional needs have been desublimated or reduced from high aspirations for aesthetic experience and social freedom and then redefined in terms that support the established reality. Community, love, and friendship, which were the promises of a higher social order contradictory to capitalism, are associated with consumer products by advertisements and made available for easy purchase. One can obtain immediate gratification through consumerism instead of through a struggle to attain sublimated forms of enjoyment. By this argument Marcuse supports the claim that capitalism is sexually repressive even in the face of the sexual revolution.

The domestication of the sexual revolution is accomplished, Marcuse argues, through a profound change in the psychic pattern of the family. The traditional authority of the father in the family has been undermined by two interrelated processes: (1) a shift toward large corporations that destroy small businesses, wiping out the property basis of patriarchy; and (2) a sweeping shift of emphasis away from the family toward the mass media, the schools, and peer groups as the child's significant others. The consequences of these transformations on child development are dramatic: 'the ego', Marcuse laments, 'shrinks to such an extent that it seems no longer capable of sustaining itself, as a self, in distinction from id and superego.[3] In Freudian terms, without the father as a focus of repression for the child's instincts, the developing individual bypasses the psychic drama of resistance to authority and therefore growth of individuality. As a personal agent of authority, the father, according to Marcuse, is in a unique relation to the child, a relation that cannot be replaced by peer groups or state agencies. The intense, intimate relation of father and child is the sole basis for later autonomy when the super-ego becomes solidified in the personality structure.

The 'fatherless society' so bemoaned by the Frankfurt School produces the conditions for fascism. Without a strong super-ego the individual is unable to resist external authority. An ambivalent relationship arises between the state and the individual, in which the latter both craves for and rebels against authority. A figure like Hitler, representing strong authority *and* rebellion against (other) authorities, perfectly matches the psychic needs of individuals socialized in the families of late capitalism.

But the other side of the story is more germane to the question of sexuality. Without patriarchy, the ego remains weak, ineffective in controlling libidinal impulses. Hence the sexual revolution. Hence also the role of advertizing in channeling desires to the benefit of the corporations. Marcuse's thesis then is that the potentials for sexual liberation, which he propounded in *Eros and Civilization*, have not emerged and indeed cannot emerge in the conditions of capitalist society.

Michael Schneider upholds the cause of Freudo-Marxism in a different way.[4] The classic anal-compulsive personality associated with the work ethic still exists in advanced capitalism, according to Schneider. The organization of labor maintains a need for people to work at rigid schedules in alienating and exploitative jobs. These people must repress their libido, deny pleasure, and save money and energy. Along with this personality type, however, advanced capitalism demands an opposite but concurrent emotional structure. Productive capacity today is so great that the economy requires continuous consumption so that capital may be reinvested in greater and greater amounts. The result is the emergence of a new personality type characterized by oral impulsiveness. One must consume on the spur of the moment; one must let oneself go, reward oneself continuously; one must buy products now, products that will yield gratification. The sexual revolution is explained by Schneider as simply another example of the oral-impulsive personality. Commodity culture makes all sexual partners equal, just as all consumer products are subject to the same standard of monetary value.

Sex is simply another impulsive act of consumption, and capitalism has tamed its radical implications. Like Marcuse, Schneider sustains the Freudo-Marxist position that the history of sexuality is made intelligible through the model of repression.

The arguments of the Freudo-Marxists raise questions that must be addressed even before considering Foucault's response to them. It must be pointed out that the position of the Freudo-Marxists, resting on the thesis of repression and its variants in the post-Victorian world, gives unwarranted support to patriarchy and undercuts the claims of feminism. The authoritarian father and his paradoxical role in fostering autonomy is the central figure of the Freudo-Marxist family romance. No doubt the position of the father in the family has been somewhat compromised due to the trends that Marcuse and Schneider indicate. But it is the middle-class father who is their reference point, even though they subscribe to a social position which, of course, relies on the agency of the working class. This confused class analysis is only the beginning of the problems with Freudo-Marxism.

More damaging is their complete denial of the progressive side of the changes in the father's position. The weakening of patriarchy leads not only to the prominence of peer groups and the media: it is the condition for the emergence of women from the constraints of the role of mother and wife. The feminism of the 1970s, which had its antecedents in the 1920s at the beginning of this process, must be seen by critical theorists and Western Marxists generally as a progressive step in the restructuring of the family and advanced capitalism in general. In addition, the widespread demands for sexual and emotional fulfillment, which Marcuse discredits, have a liberative aspect. What the Freudo-Marxists see as a weakened ego and a proto-fascist super-ego may also be interpreted as a new psychic formation in which traditional repressions are no longer valid. The relative collapse of the anal personality augurs the emergence of individuals who will not suffer silently the emotional scarcity of classical capitalism or its pseudo-fulfillment through the commodities of rich capitalism. The needs for love and community which were at the heart of the socialist dreams of the nineteenth century may become paramount political questions in the future, not on the placards of the proletariat but on those of feminists, gay liberationists and others not inured to the repressions of the nuclear family. At the very least, one can argue that the necessary data have not been tabulated or even investigated. There need to be studies of the precise nature of personality development through the first three stages of the child's life in the context of 'fatherless' families. Until that is done, all talk of the collapse of the autonomous individual remains an empty jeremiad.

That is the way things stood on the question of a theory and history of sexuality until the publication of Foucault's *The History of Sexuality*.[5] Foucault has attempted to redefine completely the question of sexuality by removing it from the paradigm of repression. Instead, sexuality for him must be considered in terms of concepts of knowledge and power. In this manner Foucault places sex in relation to the emergence of the administered society of the twentieth century. He challenges both Marx and Freud by shifting the grounds of the debate: the concepts of labor and repression no longer serve in the critical comprehension of history; the privileged places in social theory and social life are not longer the factory and the unconscious. Foucault suggests nothing less than a basic reconceptualization of the logic of history, one that promises to revitalize critical theory. It must be pointed out, however, that Foucault and Marcuse are in agreement on one fundamental point: that the alleged sexual revolution of the 1960s was not a true liberation. While Marcuse dismisses the sexual revolution as mere repressive desublimation, Foucault treats it as an extension of the profusion of discourses on sexuality.

The *History of Sexuality* provides an arena in which my

view of Foucault's work can be assessed. Foucault promised six volumes devoted to the topic. In 1976 the introductory first book appeared with the subtitle *The Will to Knowledge*, a transparent allusion to Nietzsche's *The Will to Power* that reveals Foucault's general theme: the relation of sex and self-knowledge to discourses on sexuality.[6]

The History of Sexuality opens with an attack on the Freudo-Marxist position. The concept of repression, Foucault charges, is a false guide to the problem of sexuality. It suggests that sex disappears in the nineteenth century, that sex was pushed out of consciousness and out of practice as the bourgeoisie came to power. Even a superficial reading of history, Foucault counters, demonstrates the opposite: that sexuality flourished as never before in the nineteenth century. This surprising assertion refers not to erotic fulfillment, but to the expansion of the discourse on sexuality. For Foucault sex cannot have been 'repressed' and at the same time talked about so much.

There is a possible confusion here on Foucault's part regarding the definition of repression in Freud. When Freud writes that contemporary Europe experienced the 'high-water mark of sexual repression', he was not referring to external prohibitions on sex. He was not merely arguing that people had coitus less often than in the past, though this might have been the case. Rather Freud's concept of repression denotes an intrapsychic phenomenon by which libidinous impulses are prevented from attaining consciousness in their direct forms. The impulses do not disappear but return under a different, often neurotic, guise. Hence, for Freud, sexuality never vanishes completely, as Foucault seems to suggest in his interpretation of the doctrine of repression. The claim that sex flourished in the nineteenth century as a form of discourse therefore does not necessarily contradict the findings of psychoanalysis. Nonetheless, Freudo-Marxists like Reich do seem to argue that the quantity of sex was diminished by dint of repression in the Victorian age.

Foucault's main argument against the doctrine of repression is that it is a false model of the relation between power and sex. Following Deleuze and Guattari in *Anti-Oedipus*, Foucault contends that the law does not act as a negative obstacle to the positive, natural drive of sex, as the doctrine of repression implies. Things happen quite differently.[7] For Foucault power is positive: it creates the form of sexuality. In his words, 'the law is what constitutes both desire and the lack on which it is predicated.'[8] This important shift in the argument requires elaboration.

Deleuze and Guattari contend that the Freudian concept of the Oedipus complex inverts the truth.[9] According to Freud, children have natural erotic drives for their parents which become repressed. *Anti-Oedipus*, however, argues that the sexual attachments of children for parents is a coding initiated by the parents which elicits the desire and then prohibits it. There are thus no natural sex drives. All sexuality is 'always already' coded by a law. The child's desire falls into the law of Oedipus and becomes shaped by it. Without citing Deleuze and Guattari, Foucault takes this model as the essence of power. But if that is so, the project of a history of sexuality cannot proceed by searching for prohibitions against sex; it must look instead to power as the creator of sexuality. Foucault provides extensive examples of such a view of power taken from the history of medicine.

Rather than treat the history of sexuality as a documentation of acts of repression. Foucault directs his attention to the operations of power. At this point he introduces the notion of discourse. He provides the following definition of discourse:

Discourses are tactical elements or blocks operating in the field of force relations: there can exist different and even contradictory discourses within the same strategy; they can, on the contrary, circulate without changing their form from one strategy to another, opposing strategy. We must not expect the discourses on sex to tell us, above all, what strategy they derive from, or what moral divisions they accompany, or what ideology – dominant or dominated – they represent: rather we must question them on the two levels of their tactical productivity (what reciprocal effects of power and knowledge they ensure) and their strategical integration (what conjunction and what force relationship make their utilization necessary in a given episode of the various confrontations that occur).[10]

In this passage Foucault defines discourse in relation to power. Discourse for him is not some idealist representation of ideas; it is, in materialist fashion, part of the power structure of society. Power relations must be understood in the structuralist manner as decentered, as a multiplicity of local situations. Discourses are important because they reveal the play of power in a given situation. They are not 'ideological representations' of class positions but acts of power shaping actively the lives of the populace. The history of sexuality must study discourses on sexuality to uncover the shapes given to it. Foucault rejects the distinction, which derives from the episteme of representation, between ideas/discourses and action/sexuality.

But the privileged place he gives to discourse does not seem justified. Perhaps one can read in the discourses on sex of the Victorian bourgeoisie – if one reads well between the lines – the shape of sexuality in society. But can one do the same for the nineteenth-century working class or for the peasantry of the precapitalist period? Foucault, of course, thinks that one can. Yet his notion of discourse seems to capture unequally the various periods of European history. As discourses on sexuality increase in frequency from the late eighteenth century onwards and reach an unprecedented deluge in our own day, discourse itself becomes more and more significant in the shaping of sexuality. In other words, Foucault's principle of selection (his focus on discourse) is better suited and gives more prominence to the recent period than the earlier one. He comes close to completing the circle by concluding that sexuality itself was more extensive in the recent period, if only because discourse on it increased. That will do fine to counter the Freudo-Marxists' argument about repression, but it will not serve as a proven fact.

Foucault would counter this argument by pointing out that he is not referring merely to printed discourse but to spoken discourse as well, and therefore the increased publication of books on sexuality is not an adequate index. This reply does not, however, dispel suspicions of bias toward the recent period, because the spoken discourse in a seventeenth-century village would still escape the historian's purview. I would contend that the focus on discourse derives its legitimacy from the broader intention of Foucault's thought — that is, from his reflexive concern to comprehend our own time, the present-day information society. Because this intention underlies his project and because it is inevitable that historians employ a theory which necessarily gives prominence to one epoch over another, Foucault's focus on discourse is not only legitimate but also desirable.

Foucault is in search of 'true discourses'. His definition of truth is not the philosopher's. He is not after the best-argued, the most logically coherent text. The documents he is after are not those of Kant and Hegel. He does not read discourses literally in order to analyze their concepts. Discourses for him are loci of power. They must be read from the vantage point not of the author or the intended audience but from the perspective of how they constitute a power relation concerning sexuality. The discourses that are valuable are not those of the most penetrating thinker, those that contain the best concept of sexuality. The level he is after is much more mundane, much closer to the pulse of social life. His discourses are those of ordinary doctors; they are the files of

clinics that treat sexual 'disorders'; they are the letters of
local priests; they are the dossiers housed in bureaucracies;
they are grant proposals for the study of sexuality; they are
the psychotherapist's file; they are the files of social welfare
agencies. At these locations, in these discourses, the play of
power and the question of sexuality reveal themselves. This
is where 'the political economy of a will to knowledge' of
sexuality is constituted.[11]

In the introductory volume of *The History of Sexuality*
Foucault offers an outline of the history of sexuality that
merits the attention of historians. The concept of discourse
leads Foucault directly to the Christian confession as the
locus of sexuality. Here he finds two phases. In the earlier
period, before the seventeenth century, the priest was concerned with what people did. The faithful were asked in
detail about their sexual *activities*. In that period sexuality
concerned the body, which was allowed certain positions and
denied others. The discourse of sexuality was rudimentary
and crude; talk, in the society, was open and frank. Foucault
mentions Erasmus, who encouraged advice to children on the
selection of prostitutes. More evidence about the sensuality
of the body in this period can be gleaned from Norbert Elias's
study of civilizing manners.[12]

With the Reformation and Counter Reformation the
discourse on sexuality takes another form. In the confession the priest begins to inquire not only about actions, but
also about intentions. Sexuality begins to be defined in terms
of the mind as well as the body. The scope of the sexual
expands to include the least thoughts and fantasies. A loqua-
ciousness about sexuality emerges. Everything must be pored
over and examined in great detail. A similar pattern of change
is discovered by Foucault in his history of crime and punishment.[13] Discourse intensifies from a concern with action and
the body to a concern with the mind and its intentions. But
the important change in the discourse of sexuality does not
take place until later, during the capitalist period. At this

time, although by no means because of the mode of production, the confession becomes scientific. Foucault offers as a hypothesis that the great alteration in sexuality occurred when the discourse on sex became a matter of science.[14] Once that happened, sexuality became a major preoccupation and began to assume its current shape.

The major example of a modern discourse on sexuality, a new scientific confessional, is of course psychoanalysis. Perhaps Foucault's major accomplishment in *The History of Sexuality* is to treat Freud as part of history, rather than to study the history of sex from a Freudian vantage point. The conceptual *point d'honneur* of the Freudo-Marxists — that Freud treats the instincts as outside society and therefore as a source of social criticism — is shorn of its scientific power. Freud's concept of the instincts becomes, in Foucault's hands, just another device to control and shape sexuality. The concept of the instincts is a power strategy by the new medical profession which allows them to inquire into sex, to explore it by the method of the 'talking cure', to examine dreams and fantasies, the recesses of the mind, in a way never before contemplated. The Freudian view of the instincts does not provide a reservoir of resistance against the ruling class. It does not promise a sexual revolution. For sexuality, to Foucault, is not something outside society waiting to burst through the layers of repression. On the contrary, by positing a sexual instinct Freud opened up a new realm for the domination of science over sexuality.

The heart of the matter for Foucault is that the history of sexuality amounts to a continuous increase, beginning in the seventeenth century, in the 'mechanisms' and 'technologies' of power. During the course of this history the locus of power shifts from the confessional to the research laboratories and clinics where sexuality is the subject of scientific investgation. Historians are directed by Foucault to explore in detail the 'true discourses' on sex generated under the sign of science. In particular he calls attention to four 'mechanisms of know-

ledge and power' on sex. These are: 'the hysterization of
women's bodies', 'the pedagogization of children's sex', 'the
socialization of procreative behavior', and 'the psychiatriza-
tion of perverse pleasure'. These mechanisms are directed at
four 'figures': hysterical women, masturbating children,
Malthusian couples, and perverse adults. Taken together,
these 'mechanisms' constitute the 'production of sexuality' in
the modern period.

Anyone familiar with the history of the nineteenth century
will be impressed by Foucault's choice of subjects. The literature on sexuality is indeed concerned with these four figures
to a very great extent. Perhaps Malthusian couples were more
prominent in France, where population growth stagnated in
the nineteenth century, than in England or Germany, where
demographic statistics were more favorable. One might
question as well Foucault's exclusion of the sexually diseased
male, since some historians think that syphilis was epidemic
in the nineteenth century. The aggressive female was another
major concern of doctors and parents. Assertive women were
thought to be driven by excessive sexual impulses, and sexual
surgery, such as infibulations and clitoridectomies, were
often recommended and performed. These topics would
serve as well as those chosen by Foucault to examine discourses on sexuality, and Foucault's selection must therefore
be regarded as somewhat arbitrary.

A thorough history of the discourses on the four figures
would not doubt produce an impressive confirmation of Foucault's thesis on the relation of knowledge and power to sex.
The figure of the masturbating child, for example, was the
subject of an extensive quasi-military campaign by doctors and
parents. Devices were designed, produced and sold to prevent
erection. Some favorites were metal rings with sharp teeth that
fitted around the penis and alarm systems that warned parents
of their child's sexual excitement.[15] In addition to these
advances in antimasturbatory technology, medical science
offered countless treatises on the dangers of onanism. These

sober men of learning foresaw the worst. They attributed to masturbation everything from acne and headaches to cancer and death.[16] Beyond doubt an impressive apparatus of knowledge and power was constructed with the misguided aim of preventing childhood masturbation.

Attention to these 'true discourses' on sexuality does not necessarily constitute a history of sexuality. It is doubtful that these figures could be generalized to serve as conceptual guides for a history of sexuality at any time other than the nineteenth century. Worse still, these figures and their attendant discourses only apply to one segment of the population in Europe and the United States. The bourgeoisie fits well into Foucault's categories, but the working class in the cities and perhaps the peasantry in the countryside do not. These latter groups were not subject to the knowledge/power of the medical and psychiatric professions; nor were they avid readers of discourses on hysterical women and perversions. Foucault might respond to the objection that his analysis does not account for class differences by pointing out that the spread of the discourse on sex through society took time to unfold. Yet the question remains how to account for class differences in the first place.

Foucault is cognizant of the importance of social class in the history of sexuality. He presents a fascinating discussion of the differences between the aristocracy and the bourgeoisie on the topic of the body.[17] For the aristocracy the body meant blood. Lineage was the all-important consideration for them. For the bourgeoisie, however, the body was instead a question of life and health. The capitalist class initiated a concern for the condition of the body, for its optimal functioning and its durability. Like the joggers and vegetarians of today, the classic bourgeoisie was obsessed with hygiene and longevity. The reckless hunting, whoring, and drinking of the aristocracy lost favor in the dismal world of industry.

For Foucault, the distinction between the aristocratic and bourgeois discourse on the body serves to strengthen his critique of the Freudo-Marxists. Far from repressing the body, he contends, the bourgeoisie devoted a great deal of attention to it. Nevertheless, while his argument is well taken, it does not really address the issue of sexuality. The bourgeois concern with the body was not an erotic one; good diet and hygiene are not the same as sensuality. The bourgeois body may have been cared for and tended better than that of the aristocracy, but it was far less a vessel of sexuality. One suspects in fact that the bourgeois attention to health was a utilitarian and economic quest. Energy for this social class was marshaled for the great battles of the market and the factory, not for the gentlemanly pursuit of a woman's favors. Although Foucault addresses the question of class and sex, he has not reached the heart of the problem.

Without an adequate theory of class sexuality, the emphasis on knowledge/power leads Foucault against himself to a totalizing view of the history of sexuality. Although he asserts that there is no 'unitary sexual politics', he does not offer a basis on which to comprehend sexuality in a given society in any way other than collectively. Discourses on sex may differ in a particular epoch, but they are the discourses of the society as a whole. Yet the history of sexuality cannot be pursued at the level of the total society. Social groups and regions differ too markedly in their sexuality to be considered together in one general framework. In the course of the last three centuries, the sexual practices of the aristocracy, peasantry, bourgeoisie, and working class differ more than they are alike. These differences simply cannot be explained on the basis of discourse.

Jacques Donzelot's *The Policing of Families*, a book that is much indebted to Foucault's work on the history of sexuality, treats the problem of class in a most satisfactory manner. Donzelot focuses on the family rather than on sex, but like Foucault he traces the complex interplay of the discourses of the human sciences and the actions of coercive institutions in shaping the practices he is concerned with. Donzelot convincingly demonstrates the differential impact of these technologies of power on each social class. The emergence of the urban industrial working class in nineteenth-century France presented the newly empowered bourgeoisie with a set of family practices that they found intolerable. Working class couples seemed to them incapable of conducting morally and hygienically sound family lives. The bourgeoisie responded to the conditions of proletarian families through a cluster of institutional and discursive means. Semi-public philanthropic institutions were established, wealthy women engaged in individual forms of assistance to the poor, rudimentary forms of sociological disciplines appeared, and finally, the state itself inaugurated public policies to deal with the problem. Donzelot sums up these activities with the term 'the tutelary complex'.

By this phrase he means to underscore the great irony of the situation. The bourgeoisie believed deeply in the private nuclear family, of the autonomy of the married couple in relation to the state. The working class did not establish families that conformed to the pattern of nuclearity. The bourgeoisie sought to help them to do so, but increasingly they were led to force them to do so, eventually by the direct intervention of the state. The state initiated welfare policies that were intended set in motion a change in working class families that would result in their autonomy. But the very fact of the state's intervention undermined the intended result: dependency not autonomy was the fate of the lower class family.

The bourgeois family set in play a very different complex of forces. If the bond that held together the working class was forged in a contest with juvenile court and other similar state agencies, the rope that held together the bourgeois family was tied to the schooling system. In schools teachers, parents and medical advisors blended a mixture of discourse/ practice that was the ideal tonic for the bourgeois family. Its chief ingredient was psychoanalysis, but pyschoanalysis of a

particular variety, one that holds tightly a certain image of
family functioning and employs that image strategically to
mollify family conflicts. Donzelot's term for this discourse/
practice is 'the regulation of images'. The bourgeois family
in crisis readjusted its internal relations by the guidelines of
psychoanalysis, parent-teacher organizations, family planning
agencies and psychotherapists. The all-important difference
between the bourgeois and working class families with
respect to the constellation of intervening discourse/practices
is that only for the bourgeoisie was the intervention initiated
by the family. The bourgeois family employed the regulation
of images to reinforce its autonomy and privacy while the
working class family was exposed to control by the state. In
both cases technologies of power were set in play, but with
very different results. The attention of Donzelot to class
differences demonstrates the interpretive force of Foucault's
categories without reducing the analysis to a Marxist totalization. The mode of production may have generated the two
classes, but it cannot explain the differential discourse/
practices of the family structures. The danger in Foucault's
project is that it treats discourses on sexuality only in relation
to society as a whole.

Foucault's account of the history of sexuality also goes
astray in overlooking the importance of the family. If the
emotional structure of the family is taken into account,
differences between classes regarding sexuality become intelligible. In the stifling air of the private bourgeois family of
the nineteenth century, where the feelings of each family
member have no outlet other than the family, the hysterical
woman, the masturbating child, the pervert, and the Malthusian couple emerge with clarity. Although sexuality in the
bourgeois family was open to the influences of medical discourses, the structure of everyday life in the family itself is
of at least equal importance in the task of explanation. If it
can be shown, as I am convinced it can, that sexual patterns
are illuminated by family structure, then reliance on the

priest, the doctor, and the psychiatrist can be given a less influential but still considerable role. Foucault's program for the history of sexuality deflects too much attention away from the family in favor of more distant agencies of power. Like Christopher Lasch's *Haven in a Heartless World*, Foucault's book draws attention to the great politics of 'true discourses' when it should focus more on the little politics of family romances.

Commentaries on Foucault's earlier works have pointed out that his concept of power is vague and ambiguous. The power embodied in discourses on sex is not the clearly defined power of the state or even the discernible power of the 'helping professions'. Power, Foucault proclaims, is everywhere.[19] In all the relations of society, power — especially the power of discourse — is exercised. Foucault is sensitive to the force of opinion on people's action. He sees clearly the way all practice is subject to the pressure of what he calls discourse. In everyday life no action is innocent; no project is carried out from the pure intention of the actor. Individual reason is not the power that determines what happens. Especially people who do not conform to dominant social values — the handicapped, racial minorities, those with unusual sexual preferences, the physically deformed — can feel the influence of what Foucault calls 'force relations' or 'technologies of power'.

The irony of Foucault's position is that although he is acutely aware of 'power relations' in society, he pays little heed to the 'power' of his own discourse. He does not pose the fundamental question, What is the role of his own discourse in the history of discourse on sexuality? If discourse is a mode of power that elicits sexuality and shapes it, will not the same fate befall Foucault's discourse? Foucault seeks to liberate society from the power of 'true discourse' on sex and thereby to contribute to the 'counterattack' of free 'bodies and pleasures'. But nothing prevents Foucault's project from becoming yet another 'true discourse'.

Three more volumes of Foucault's *The History of Sexuality* have recently appeared and the degree to which the project can attain the success of *Discipline and Punish* will depend on the response to these books.[20] In the years since the first instalment of *The History of Sexuality* Foucault has presented to the public, in the form of addresses and articles, indications of the line of research they pursue.[21] In these pieces one theme emerges clearly: Foucault has shifted the focus of the project. The first volume centers on sexuality as it is constituted through discourse/practice. The recent work places the subject at the center of the analysis, subordinating sexuality to the role of the theme through which the subject can be grasped. In the West, Foucault maintains, subjects have come to recognize themselves, to find their 'truth', in their sexuality. Foucault gives several alternative formulations of his new direction. He speaks of his field of interest as 'the politics of the true' or as 'a genealogy of ethics.' The phrase that probably indicates best his current project is 'techniques of the self'. He is studying those discourse/practices by which the individual gives shape to his or her own subjectivity.

With this change Foucault occupies a territory that he had earlier placed off limits: the subject. He is studying the interiority of the individual, the terrain of existentialists, phenomenologists, psychoanalysts – all those philosophies of consciousness that he earlier rejected for their humanist illusions. The difference between Foucault and Sartre is seemingly narrowed. Foucault applauds Sartre for avoiding 'the idea of the self as something which is given to us'.[22] Sartre, Foucault writes, has a 'theoretical insight to the practice of creativity.' Foucault too will study the self-constitution of the subject. But Sartre went astray with the criterion of authenticity which dictates too much about the relation one has with oneself. Instead, Foucault prefers a more open approach, one that will 'relate the kind of relation he has to himself to a creative activity'.[23]

Foucault's analysis of the subject takes on the question of

the centered subject more directly than ever before. *The History of Sexuality* undercuts the attempt to ontologize any view of the subject (the *cogito*, authenticity, libido) by demonstrating the historicity of the forms of subjectivity as well as the means through which subjectivity is constituted. In a sense Foucault's project is more radical than those that would deny intelligibility to the subject. He carries the Nietzschean critique of 'truth' probably as far as it can go. Truth is studied as a constituted, historical multiplicity, not at the level of philosophical doctrine but at the level of subjective self-constitution. The truth about oneself emerges as the result of a complexity of discourses and practices, one that varies in fundamental ways at different times and among different social groups.

The History of Sexuality abandons the safe terrain of modern history and goes back to the period between the 4th Century BC and the early Middle Ages. Foucault notes that during this period the sexual code did not vary greatly: the same basic prohibitions were in place. Laws restricted sexual activity to the married couple and in general discouraged excess because of its alleged danger to health. The techniques of the self, however, altered drastically. Among the male ruling class in the Ancient period, sexual practice related to an art of living. Sex was separate from religious matters and from social institutions in general. The issue of which sexual acts to practice was decided on the basis of personal ethics. Sex was an active experience through which the beautiful life was sought. Homosexual love between a man and boy presented a difficulty for the man, since the boy was not able to provide full reciprocity in the relationship, a reciprocity necessary for the best possible life.

With Christianity the relationship of sex to techniques of the self changed in character. Sexual practice was connected directly with religious experience. Sex was a matter of the passive flesh not the active body as it was for the Ancients. The male erection was an involuntary incursion by the flesh on the soul. Sex was a unique vice for Christians like Joannes Cassianus (ca. 370– ca. 435). It was the only sin of the flesh that resembled sins of the soul like pride. The struggle against it was unremitting and deep. 'It is a question of destroying completely an impulse whose suppression does not lead to the death of the body. Among the eight vices, fornication alone is at once innate, natural and corporal in its origin.'[24] The Christian subject had to constitute itself through techniques that would eradicate completely all sexual impulses. Sex was the great testing ground of the Christian soul. The ultimate standard of faith was the absence of 'erotic dreams and nocturnal pollution'. When that was attained, the subject was free of heteronomous influences.

Christain faith elicited techniques of the self that constituted the truth of the subject at a more interior level than the Ancients. Christian sexual practices set in motion a movement toward 'subjectivization' in relation to 'a process of knowledge that obliged one to look for and to tell the truth about oneself.'[25] In the monk's vow of chastity and in the confessional, Christianity established two sets of practices directed toward the constitution of the truth of the subject in relation to sex. Restrictive sexual codes were only the remote horizon of Christian practices; at the center was the interminable examination of one's conscience for indications of danger.

The parallel is striking between Foucault's depiction of the contrast between the Ancients and the Christians and Nietzsche's. For Nietzsche, the master morality of the Ancients with its distinction between good and bad was a direct, simple expression of the will to power. The slave morality of the Christians with its distinction between good and evil was a complex, indirect expression mediated through the poison of resentment. The deeper, more interiorized morality of the Christians was a consequence in part of its connection with the religious issues of death and of God. Similarly Foucault discovers the key to the Christian technique of the self in the raising of the stakes over sex by relating it to religious issues. For both Nietzsche and Foucault, the question of the truth about oneself becomes a more rigorous and urgent issue in the Christian period. Differences between the two genealogists are also important: Foucault's focus on the techniques of the self through discourse/practice is more amenable to concrete historical analysis than Nietzsche's philological method and concept of the will to power.

The implications of Foucault's project for the modern period are arresting. During the Enlightenment the religious dimension of the techniques of the self dissipate. A medico-scientific framework takes over the same set of discourse/practices, developing them further and culminating perhaps in psychoanalysis.[26] The scientific method of constituting the truth of the self in sex uncomfortably resembles the Christian counterpart. But the full statement of this position requires a full analysis of the recently published volumes which is inappropriate here.

NOTES

1. See especially 'Dialectical Materialism and Psychoanalysis'. in *Sex-Pol Essays, 1929–1934*, ed. Lee Baxandall (New York: Vintage 1966). For a clear summary of Reich's thought and that of other Freudo-Marxists, see Paul Robinson, *The Freudian Left* (New York: Harper and Row, 1969). Also interesting is Reuben Osborn, *Marxism and Psychoanalysis* (New York: Delta 1965).
2. Much of Marcuse's writing is on this topic. See *Eros and Civilization: A Philosophical Inquiry into Freud* (New York: Vintage 1962); *One-Dimensional Man* (Boston: Beacon Press, 1964); *An Essay on Liberation* (Boston: Beacon Press, 1969); and *Five Lectures* (Boston: Beacon Press, 1970).
3. Herbert Marcuse, 'The Obsolescence of the Freudian Concept of Man', in *Five Lectures*, trans. J. Shapiro and S. Weber (Boston: Beacon Press, 1970), p. 57.
4. Michael Schneider, *Neurosis and Civilization: A Marxist/Freudian Synthesis*, trans. Michael Roloff (New York: Urizen, 1975). Also

of interest is Reimut Reiche, *Sexuality and Class Struggle*, trans. Susan Bennett (London: New Left Books, 1970).

5. *The History of Sexuality*, vol. 1, *An Introduction*, trans. Robert Hurley (New York: Pantheon, 1978). The French title is *Histoire de la sexualité*, 1, *La Volonté de savoir* (Paris: Gallimard, 1976).

6. For interesting commentaries on Foucault see Edward Said, *Beginnings: Intention and Method* (Baltimore: Johns Hopkins University Press, 1975) and 'The Problem of Textuality: Two Exemplary Positions', *Critical Inquiry* 4, No. 4 (Summer, 1978), pp. 673–714; David Carroll, 'The Subject of Archaeology, or the Sovereignty of the Episteme', *Modern Language Notes* No. 93 (1978), pp. 695–722; and Hayden White, 'Foucault De-coded', *History and Theory* 12, No. 1 (1971), pp. 23–54.

7. Gilles Deleuze and Félix Guattari, *L'Anti-Oedipe: Capitalisme et schizophrénie* (Paris: Editions de Minuit, 1972).

8. *The History of Sexuality*, p. 81.

9. See Mark Poster, *Critical Theory of the Family* (New York: Seabury, 1978) for a further discussion of the position of Deleuze and Guattari.

10. *The History of Sexuality*, pp. 101–2.

11. Ibid, p. 73.

12. Norbert Elias, *The Civilization Process* (New York: Urizen, 1978).

13. *Discipline and Punish.*

14. *The History of Sexuality*, p. 65.

15. Stephen Kern, 'Explosive Intimacy: Psychodynamics of the Victorian Family', *History of Childhood Quarterly* 1, No. 3 (1974), pp. 437–62.

16. For examples of this discourse, see René A. Spitz, 'Authority and Masturbation'. *Psychoanalytic Quarterly*, No. 21 (1952), pp. 90–527.

17. *The History of Sexuality*, pp. 122–5.

18. Jacques Donzelot *The Policing of Families*, trans. Robert Hurley (New York: Pantheon, 1979, French edition 1977).

19. *The History of Sexuality*, p. 93.

20. Recently are: Volume 2, *L'Usage des plaisirs* (Paris: Gallimard, 1984), on Greek and Roman sexuality; Volume 3, *Le Souci de soi* (Paris: Gallimard, 1984), on early Christianity and the confessional; and a separate collection of essays, entitled *Les Aveux de la chair* (Paris: Gallimard, 1984), on the technology of the self in the first two centuries AD.

21. Of these I have consulted 'Usage des plaisirs et techniques de soi', *Le Débat*, 27 (November, 1983), pp. 46–72 which is presented as the 'general introduction' to the next three volumes; 'Le Combat de la chasteté' *Communications*, 35 (1982), pp. 15–25, introduced as 'an extract' from Volume 3 (I am indebted to Judy Fiskin for calling my attention to this piece); 'The History of Sexuality: Interview' with Bernard-Henri Lévy, trans. in *Oxford Literary Review*, Vol. 4, No. 2 (1980), pp. 3–14; and 'How We Behave', interview with Hubert Dreyfus and Paul Rabinow in *Vanity Fair* (November, 1983), pp. 61–9, which appears as part of the promotional activities associated with the appearance of the new volumes. I also obtained tapes of two talks by Foucault: 'Sexuality and Solitude', New York University (November, 1980) and 'The Birth of Biophysics', Princeton University (November, 1980).
22. 'How We Behave', p. 64.
23. Ibid.
24. 'Le Combat de la chasteté', p. 17.
25. Ibid., p. 23.
26. 'How We Behave', p. 67.

6

Foucault and the Mode of Information: An Assessment

Foucault offers historians a new framework for studying the past (knowledge/power), a new set of methods for doing so (archeology and genealogy), and a new notion of temporality (discontinuity). Suggestive as it is, this theory of history is burdened with several difficulties.

One objection often raised to Foucault's writing is that it is difficult, mannered, and finally incomprehensible. Empiricists and Marxists, this position maintains, at least have the virtue of readability. Such an objection would raise serious questions if it could be shown that Foucault's obscurity derives from a fuzziness or confusion of thought. I would argue that the difficulty can be explained instead by the novelty of Foucault's theory of history, by his anti-evolutionist, anti-subjectivist strategies which go deeply against the grain of practitioners of the human sciences.[1]

A more serious charge concerns the unsatisfying incompleteness of Foucault's position. In order to avoid the problems of Marxism and empiricism, Foucault refused to totalize his position, refuses to present a neat and closed theory of history, a formula that would explain the past. He doggedly takes each question separately, exploring its details and specificities, acknowledging that there are gaps in history, unmapped continents of experience. He does not try in all cases to show connections between diverse phenomena, explain ideas by reference to the economy, a revolution by a fiscal crisis or a war. In the book on prisons he traces the new technologies of power associated with its birth but does not mention how specific events shaped that birth, nor how the new panoptic prison system was diffused in the nine-teenth and twentieth centuries. The syncopated, uneven character of his books rubs unpleasantly against the sensi-bilities of those expecting a text that resolves all the main questions.

There is indeed a difficulty with Foucault's method of procedure. Without a systematic theory Foucault cannot explain why he does not explore questions he has omitted from his text. He permits himself to trace the changing forms of power/knowledge without, for example, dis-cussing the response of victims of this process. He does not ask, in *Discipline and Punish*, how the prisoners reacted to the disciplinary constraints of Panopticism. He describes minutely the efficiency and thoroughness of the prison system, its complete control over the individual, its relent-less supervision of the least detail of activity. He then re-veals that the Panopticon, judged by its intention of reform and normalization of the prison population, has been a scandalous failure. Recidivism rates have always been high. But without an account of the response of the prisoners to the system, the 'failure' of the system sits in his text like an uninvited guest.

Foucault does argue that this 'hypocrisy' of the prison system is only a ruse, that the technology of power it es-tablishes is its only real purpose, and that propaganda about the reform of criminals is merely an ideological decoy. Nevertheless, in interviews beginning in 1977, he does begin to acknowledge the importance of resistance to structures.[2] He admits that history must delineate not only the coloni-zation of everyday life by knowledge/power but the count-less revolts that accompany it.[3] Does this mean that Foucault is shifting to a dialectical approach? Further, can one discuss resistance without resorting to traditional notions of the subject and freedom? In short, how can one develop a theory of resistance without falling back into the problems that plague the Marxist ideas of class consciousness and the proletariat as revolutionary agent? Suffice it is to say that much work remains to be done before this difficult issue can be properly addressed.

Moreover, Foucault's unsystematic discourse leads to problems at the epistemological level of the formation of concepts. Like Nietzsche, Foucault introduces his categories in the midst of his text, without a full elaboration or a systematic presentation. For example, the concept of 'the technology of power', a central theme of *Discipline of Punish*, appears first on page 23 with no explanation whatsoever. Foucault is there discussing the 'four general rules' of the book. The third rule reads as follows:

> 3. Instead of treating the history of penal law and the history of the human sciences as two separate series whose overlapping appears to have had on one or the other, or perhaps on both, a disturbing or useful effect, according to one's point of view, see whether there is not some common matrix or whether they do not both derive from a single process of 'epistemological-juridical' formation: in short, make the technology of power the very principle both of the humanization of the penal system and of the knowledge of man.[4]

In this off-hand manner Foucault specifies the object of his study as 'the technology of power' of the prison systems from the Old Regime to the present. But what does it mean to say that one will 'make the technology of power' the principle of both the institution of the prison and the social science that studies it? Foucault employs the term 'technology of power' dozens of times in the book; he also uses other terms as if they were synonyms ('micro-physics of power', 'mechanisms of power' and so forth). At issue is not the game of finding all the meanings of the term 'technology of power' in order to show a contradiction in Foucault's thought or simply to refine a formal definition of the term. The difficulty lies elsewhere: without a clearly enunciated systematic theory the limits of Foucault's project remain uncertain. It is impossible to indicate the parameters of the phenomenon of the technology of power, for instance, without a systematic elaboration of its conceptual basis. By the end of the book, the reader may have a pretty good notion of what Foucault means by the technology of power, but it will be very difficult indeed to determine if the category is compatible with other theories, such as Marxism, or if it can be the basis of studies of other institutional matrices. In fact, Foucault's tendency to totalize the concept 'technology of power', going against the grain of his general position, can be attributed to his failure adequately to theorize it.

Foucault's theoretical diffidence is the consequence of his standpoint on the human sciences. He adamantly rejects the traditional strategy of theoretical development and empirical verification that is practiced by liberal positivists and Marxists alike. In the *German Ideology* Marx insisted that the value of the theory of the mode of production could be determined only by empirical studies.[5] What Foucault finds objectionable in standard social science is the unacknowledged implication of the claim of knowledge, that is, the will to power. Like the Frankfurt School's critique of humanism in the *Dialectic of the Enlightenment* and, of course, like Nietzsche in *Beyond Good and Evil*,[6] Foucault argues that systematic social science, especially careful theoretical elaboration, contains within itself an element of domination of a technology of power. As was stated in the passage above where the term 'technology of power' was introduced, the discourse of criminology is itself a form of power. Technologies of power consist of knowledge and practice intimately associated in the creation of social relations based on domination. Because social science is not neutral, above the fray of class struggles, the rational exercise of theoretical production is implicated in the problem of domination. And Marxism, with its oppressive state systems and hierarchical political parties is not different in principle form the behavioral sciences and policy sciences of capitalism. Even if the theorist explicitly takes the side of the oppressed rather than hiding behind the mask of scientific neutrality, the function of domination associated with systematic theory is not eliminated.

In *Discipline and Punish* Foucault is by and large consistent in his theoretical asceticism. Many readers find the book frustrating and difficult because at the same time that the case is made against modern prison systems, nothing is offered by the author as a response to it. Students of the book find in it an impression of deep despair[7] created by the convincing genealogy of prisons without the utopian alternative that systematic theory provides. If the concept of the technology of power were fully elaborated at some point, a political stance of refusal would have to emerge. Forms of resistance to the technology of power, so underplayed by Foucault in *Discipline and Punish* (see his acknowledgement of this problem in *Knowledge/Power*), are a necessary concomitant of a standard theory.[8] Marx theorized a proletarian revolt against capitalism and liberals theorized resistance to monarchical despotism. But if such a theoretical turn were taken, Foucault contends, the concept of technology of power would return to the theorist and become an emanation of the reason of the author, Foucault himself. The author of the theory would be the commander of a new movement and would exercise domination over its followers. The intellectual would take his place at the head of the revolutionary column; his mind would be venerated by the oppressed as a source of power and they would be subject to oppression by him. Once again the scenario of the Western philosophical tradition would be enacted as Hegel's deity of reason would confirm its dialectical power of immanence.

Foucault's refusal of systematic theory is thus similar to Nietzsche's suspicion of reason as the center of being. And he gives up much to maintain that stance. He insists that his books are only tools for the revolutionary deconstruction of the established apparatus.[9] Or he would have us to think of them as bombs for others to throw at the halls of power and wealth. The only systematic principle for this anti-systematic writer is his denial of system, denial of reason, and consequently denial of authorship.[10] Yet even if one sympathizes with Foucault's predicament, the position he is in remains a predicament, one frought with difficulties.[11]

In addition to the refusal to systematize his position, there is another side to Foucault's theoretical timidity, one that also raises doubts and causes concern. Foucault is an historian of discourse above all else. He argues for the power effects of knowledge rather than its truth value. He is acutely aware of the way discourse shapes practice, the way knowledge is a material force in history. Yet he declines to differentiate his own discourse from that of others. He argues brilliantly that psychoanalysis, for example, is a discourse on sexuality that takes control of it and produces it in new forms. He urges us to rid ourselves of such 'true discourses' on sexuality, but he does not provide a theoretical basis for distinguishing between discourses that lead to domination and those that pave the way for liberation. He never mediates on the power effect of his own discourse or provides criteria by which one can distinguish its conservative and radical modes.

Foucault attempts to defend himself against charges of inadequate epistemological self-reflection by maintaining that writers never attain an understanding of the assumptions that inform their work. 'It is not possible', Foucault wrote in *The Archeology of Knowledge*, 'for us to describe our own archive, since it is from within these rules that we speak, since it is that which gives to what we can say . . . its modes of appearance.'[12] Both *The Order of Things* and *The Archeology of Knowledge* argue with great persuasiveness that the rules of formation of any discourse are beneath the writer's awareness. Surely then Foucault himself cannot be asked to do what he has demonstrated others could not do. Although there is much to be said for this argument, it is finally not convincing because it speaks only to the textual level itself, the text as a system of signifiers, leaving aside the question of the text as practice, of discourse as truth effects. When the connection is made between knowledge and power, discourse and practice, as Foucault began to do in the works that followed *The Archeology of Knowledge*, the epistemological question shifts its ground and becomes available for self-reflection, at least partially. If pure epistemology – the principles of apodicticity – is a false question, the power of truth is not, and one must be prepared to explore the way one's own discourse enters the world and disturbs it.

Discipline and Punish cannot escape its fate as a form of communication. However much Foucault would hide from his text, withdraw his rational authorship, and however sound his reasons for doing so, his text remains itself a discourse and as a discourse it retains its power-effects. To deny them is not to make them disappear. Foucault's confusion is therefore to think that his awareness of the limits of reason and systematic theory can result in a form of theory immune from those limits. In short, Foucault betrays an idealist assumption that an author's awareness of the dilemmas of authorship sanctions a stance of non-authorship. In other words, that Foucault himself, in his writing, can elude the technology of power of writing. But it is clear that if the domination inherent in reason and authorship can be muted, that would occur not through an author's awareness but through a change in the social system, a new set of practices in which the audience and the system of publishing no longer conferred power on the author, a situation that has never existed and may never exist. For these reasons the discourse of the technology of power must be considered badly incomplete and therefore open to abuse. Thus at both ends of the theoretical spectrum there are unresolved problems: Foucault neither theorizes systematically the field of history nor examines epistemologically the basis of his thought.

Foucault defends himself against charges of inadequate systematization of theory by challenging the traditional notion of the intellectual. At least since the Enlightenment, Western culture has supported the intellectual as the defender of natural rights, the advocate of humanity, the representative of the universal. Foucault rightly names Voltaire as the typical case. The intellectual was the advance guard of progress and revolution, the solvent of traditional beliefs and entrenched authority. So accepted was this view of the intellectual that the ultraconservative Joseph de Maistre could attribute the fall of the Old Regime to two of them: Voltaire and Rousseau. In the twentieth century the position of the intellectual has been questioned provocatively by Julien Benda, Antonio Gramsci, and others – Benda accusing them of cultural treason, Gramsci distinguishing traditional and organic types. Yet Foucault has little difficulty placing Marx in the line of the Enlightenment *philosophe*. Did he not locate the universal interest of man in the cause of the working class, ignoring completely the interests of women, children, and the non-European world? Did he not arrogate to himself the position of science and the ability to discriminate between the true and false consciousness of laboring men? These are irrefutable signs that Marx was an intellectual of the classic type.

Foucault terms that personage a 'general' intellectual and distinguishes him from a 'specific' intellectual. The specific intellectual is a creature of the twentieth century with its fragmentation of knowledge, its multiplication of disciplines, its infinite expansion of research centers, its explosion of the printed word, its professionalization of discourse. Today anyone who claims to speak for the universal interests of man appears arrogant or naive, utopian or mad. Marxists especially have bemoaned the splintering of knowledge and the loss of stature of the intellectual. They have not overlooked the conservative implications of the rampant professionalism in the social sciences. When fields of knowledge splinter into fragments, no one has the stature to speak for the interests of society as a whole, to criticize the system, or to represent the universal. There is no secret about who benefits from this development. The ruling class discredits its gadflies as cranks who do not have enough information to evaluate the situation. The shift from intellectual to expert, from social critic to sociological specialist, undercuts the task of radical theory. Or so the Marxists think.

Foucault finds a brighter side to these developments. Especially since May 1968, the locus of contestation has moved from the general to the specific. Criminals challenge the prison; asylum inmates, attendants, and therapists disrupt the hospital; welfare workers and clients protest against the bureaucracy; housewives and consumers organize against the corporations; community residents march against the spread of nuclear generators; minority groups contest the injustices of the legal system. The revolution proceeds not against the state and capitalism; it is fueled not by the parties and the unions; but at the local level, in concrete situations, in particular institutions, it moves unexpectedly this way and that without apparent logic. This scenario is like that in the concept of the *rhizome* of Deleuze and Guattari, where social order is undermined by a nomadic guerrilla tactic that is impervious to attack. Thus Foucault celebrates the demise of the traditional intellectual and the rise of a new breed of radical protesters. By speaking only for themselves and their local situation, the specific intellectuals raise effective arms, Foucault thinks, against 'the microphysics of power'.

In 1971—72 Foucault participated in a movement called the Prison Information Group (GIP), which organized for prison reform. The practice of GIP exemplified the new role of the specific intellectual. Like Guattari in his protest against mental institutions, Foucault did not pretend to speak for the prisoners, to name their discontents, to become the subject of their oppression. Instead GIP, manipulating the celebrity of its members, helped to create a space in which the voice of the prisoners could be heard. By marching outside the prison walls, GIP members lured the attention of the media to the problems of prisoners but refused to speak in their names. In this way the prisoners' protest could not be squelched by the adminstrators with impunity, because the population in general had been alerted to the deplorable conditions of prison life.

If it is granted that the specific intellectual uncovers sources of radicalism outside the workplace, it remains unclear in Foucault's discourse how protest against the technology of power can be effective. While marvelling at the insights of *Discipline and Punish*, readers conclude pessimistically that the new discipline of knowledge and power that spreads so extensively throughout the social space is more effective than capitalism and more ominous than imperialism.[13]

The limitations of Foucault's self-consciousness extend farther to the question of reference or situation. Foucault does not interrogate, as Marx did, the conditions of his own thought. He never asks about the historical conjuncture in which he raises questions. There is an absence of reflexiveness in his texts that is disturbing, one that transcends the supposed inability to analyze one's own archive. For Marx the existence of the proletariat and the capitalist mode of production were the conditions for the development of socialist theory. Similarly for Foucault, one can ask: What are the social conditions for a theory to emerge and maintain that history is a morphology of knowledge/power?

The strategy behind asking the question of the social

context of Foucault's discourse is not to reduce the meaning of his text to the social level. Marx's thought, for example, was not 'determined by' industrial revolution, but found its power and its limits in its self-conscious insertion in the social field. Marx adopted the standpoint of the proletariat thereby at once limiting the claims to truth of his discourse and connecting it politically to the historical conjuncture. A parallel strategy can be followed in relation to Foucault's texts.

At issue is the question of totalization. In the first chapter I compared Foucault's position to Sartre's. I argued that Foucault was right to reject totalization at the ontological or analytical level. The field of analysis must remain open and unbounded. The theorist can only propose the analysis of specific features of the social field, perhaps drawing connections between those features and other levels but no more than that. The totality remains a horizon of thought, never its object. I also argued that at the epistemological or interpretive level a moment of totalization was desirable and unavoidable. At the pre-theoretical level, before the object of investigation is established or the categories developed, the theorist makes a choice. This choice concerns a political judgement about what is important in the present conjuncture, about what needs to be done, about the theorist's relation to his or her world and the relation of the theorist's work to this world. At this moment of theory formulation a form of totalization is implicit if not explicit. The problem with Foucault's discourse in *Discipline and Punish* and *The History of Sexuality* rests in large measure with the absence of epistemological totalization. Rarely in these texts does the reader find any mention of the present conjuncture as a hermeneutical source of the text.

From the standpoint of Foucault's own strategy of placing sharp limits on reason, of insisting on the interrelation of power and knowledge, of undermining all claims to absolute, universal truth, the lack of self-reflexivity makes no sense. The most salutory method for Foucault to forestall universalist truth claims in his own text is to situate his own position and make finite his own assertions, in short to acknowledge and make explicit his own role as a specific intellectual. In the texts I have examined here Foucault never once gives a shape to his standpoint in the present conjuncture. The figure of the specific intellectual is not one that Foucault applies to himself. In interviews and talks Foucault suggests that his texts may be employed as tools, as '*offres de jeu*', in the task of struggling against domination. He never elaborates the relation between the specific intellectual, one involved directly in combat against domination, and the writer who assembles tools for that combat. It can be argued that what I referred to as a lack of systematization in Foucault's position derives from his refusal to totalize his thought at the epistemological level and elaborate the relation between his discourse and his possible role as a specific intellectual.

The irony in all of this is that self-reflexivity furthers not undermines Foucault's anti-rationalist animus. Since the task of contextualization is consonant with Foucault's main intellectual strategy and since its elaboration would strengthen the case for his position, I will attempt to provide that analysis in the concluding pages.

Two dangers need to be avoided. First, I am not imagining Foucault's intentions. I am not substituting myself in the place of Foucault and through imaginative reconstitution inventing the totalization that informs his personal relation to the world. What I intend is to locate the possible connections between the texts *Discipline and Punish* and *The History of Sexuality* and the present conjuncture. From the perspective of critical social theory I am interested in the strengths of Foucault's texts, not in his consciousness. I seek further to clarify a theoretical stance, not enter someone's mind. Second, the results will be partial. The relations

I seek to outline between the texts and the world do not form a completely unified whole. They are fragmentary and suggestive rather than final and closed.

There are three lines of intersection between Foucault's texts and the present conjuncture which both confirm the significance of those texts and improve the position of critical theory: (1) the concept of discourse in general and the critique of reason and absolute forms of rationality, and (3) the mode of information. I will discuss each of these lines of intersection in turn.

The first issue may be posed bluntly. Why is the question of discourse pertinent? There is one place, during an interview with the *Esprit* group, that Foucault does raise this question:

> There exists today a problem which is not without importance for political practice: the problem of the laws, of the conditions of exercise, of functioning, of the institutionalization of scientific discourses. That's what I have undertaken to analyze historically — by choosing the discourses which have, not the strongest epistemological structure . . . but the densest and most complex field of positivity.[14]

While recognizing the problem, Foucault does not pursue it at any great length. If he had, he would have been able to argue that the contemporary role of the human sciences authorizes — or better compels — critical social theory to adopt a standpoint from which discourse/practice, 'truth' and modes of domination, are problematized and analysed historically.

At the center of the task of critical social theory is the effort to conceptualize and empirically demonstrate the historicity of contemporary modes of domination. This aim differentiates critical theory from 'scientific' sociology, the latter being content with the measurement and explanation of social phenomena. Critical theory, on the contrary, with its method of historical reconstruction, undermines the appearance of naturalness of modes of domination, a naturalness that scientific sociology, regardless of the intentions of its practitioners, tends to confirm. Marx accomplished the task of critical social theory perhaps to a degree never equalled before or since by demonstrating the historicity and specifying the mechanisms of domination inherent in industrial capitalism. However, he fell back into the ideological mode of liberal political economy by framing the advances of his position in terms of liberal norms, i.e., universal emancipation. After revealing the inability of liberal political revolution to achieve democracy (classless society), he went on to argue that the proletarian social revolution could accomplish that end. The metaphysic of the complete abolition of domination reinserted itself within critical theory.

A chief objective of this book has been to show that Foucault has accomplished a task similar to that of Marx, but without much of the accompanying metaphysical baggage. Foucault's analysis of prisons and sexuality historicizes contemporary phenomena, undermining their naturalness, and specifies the mechanisms of domination inherent in them (the Panopticon and true discourses). This is a tremendous achievement from the perspective of critical social theory. Yet it is an achievement won at the cost of abandoning many of the theoretical positions of Marx and Western Marxism. In order to grasp the specific mechanisms of domination inherent in the phenomena of prisons and sexuality Foucault adopts a Nietzschean strategy of genealogy oriented to discontinuity, to the differential play of power relations in the historical phenomena; a post-structuralist strategy of detotalization oriented to the particularity of the phenomena; and a structuralist strategy oriented to remove the analysis from the register of subjectivist humanism. Each of the three strategies effected a tactical reversal of the metaphysical field in which critical theory had been inscribed. The first two strategies have received enough attention in earlier chapters; the third merits another look.

From liberal and Marxist perspectives discourses about society have the intention of furthering emancipation. Knowledge promotes freedom. This basic assumption characterizes discourse since the Enlightenment. A serious problem arises, however, when it can be shown that such discourses become organized into disciplinary institutions, both in the West and the East, and begin to exert powerful shaping influences (not unlike domination) on the social field. The examples Foucault provides are criminology and psychoanalysis. (In studies before 1968 he demonstrated similar effects regarding medicine and psychiatry.) The human sciences project 'man' as their object and, with the intention of liberating that object, begin to control it in a manner not unlike that of the natural sciences.

The problem has a double source. First, the subjectivist object 'man' and second, the objectivist subject 'reason'. To conceptualize the object 'man' one necessarily gives it a shape, one creates one's object in a metaphysical act similar to the account in Genesis. For examples of this procedure one need only turn to the Marxist concept of the proletariat or the liberal concept of economic man. Shades of Stakhanov and Robinson Crusoe pervade the pages of the most distinguished academic journals. Foucault attempts to sidestep this conceptual impasse by systematically 'objectivizing the object'. He takes discourse/practices as they appear in their textuality and 'micro-physics of power' without resorting to a subject who would act behind them, author them, be responsible for them, cause them. He concentrates on the internal regularities of these objects, ferreting out their mechanisms of domination. He does not have to ask what is the relation between discourses or ideas and practices or behaviors, because that distinction itself is rooted in the Cartesian dualism that is the substance of the notion of 'man' in the human sciences.

The second problem in the human sciences concerns assumptions about the scientiest or scholar, the subject of knowledge. Here the difficulty is greater with liberalism, positivism and official Marxism than it is with Western Marxism. As long as reason is posited as a neutral tool, or as one that can only promote freedom, the power effects of reason are obscured, masked and legitimated. Long ago Descartes wrote in effect that if the world does not conform to reason, so much the worse for the world. Reason orders reality, but at the same time insists that it has no obscuring influence on its object. No doubt cognitive activity (reason) is necessary for theoretical and scientific work. Yet the tendency in the human sciences is to inflate the scope and reality of reason into an originating principle that becomes the end, not just the means, of generating discourses. If reason in some form is the neutral or freedom-promoting origin of the human sciences, the intellectual becomes a universal figure either at the head of the revolutionary van-guard or the pinnacle of the social hierarchy. To avoid the dangers of the surreptitious power of reason Foucault refuses to systematize his position, to organize his work into coherent categories which through their logical impeccability alone command adherence.

The criticism of Foucault that one finds repeated most often is that the term 'power', as he employs it, is too vague and unlocalized. If power is everywhere, the critics contend, the prospect for democratization is slim. Foucault's analysis according to this view leads to pessimism or quietism, a sort of apolitical stance advocated by the notorious 'new philo-sophers'. While this charge is serious enough, it can be made even more substantial by associating it with Foucault's formu-lation of the problem of domination. The 'technologies of power' shape practices and constitute modes of domination. Modes of domination can be overturned, as happened to the 'torture' system of punishment of the Old Regime. But in Foucault's writings, new modes of domination always seem to replace old ones, just as the Pantopicon emerged in the nineteenth century. Not only is power omnipresent in Foucault's discourse, but the impression is left that history is a sucession of modes of domination, a Sisyphean tale of endless technologies of power, of an interminable struggle against domination.

Indeed, Foucault has a strong determination not to privilege the present social formation, not to allow the least trace of progressivism to appear in his text. This tendency leads some critics to view him as a pessimist, as has been mentioned before. At the same time it can be argued that another interpretation of his work is equally plausible and in fact preferable. If one rejects evolutionist progressivism because of its tendency to legitimize the present, the reasonable alternative is to focus on the limitations of all social formations. Such a strategy does not rule out a critical perspective that opposes domination; it simply reduces the promises of radical change. The existing form of domination is the one that is oppressive and must be resisted, even if there is no guarantee that a new form of domination will not arise to replace the old. The vision that emerges out of Foucault's writing is not necessarily pessimism, but it is one shorn of the dream of 'solving the riddle of history', of ending class society forever, of ridding the world once and for all of tyrants. To reject evolutionism is only to reject teleology, not the possibility of democratizing change. The notion of power in Foucault is inchoate and the notion of domination pervasive because reason cannot legislate the finiteness of power or the limit of domination. It can do no more than point to specific instances of each and make them intelligible so they may better be resisted. To argue otherwise, to think that reason can represent domination in its essence, place it in a conceptual basket and hand it over to the oppressed in a neat bundle, is to inflate reason beyond its inherent limitations.

And yet certainly the concepts of power and domination in Foucault are not without their difficulties. For Foucault goes so far in limiting the scope of reason that he is conceptually unable to distinguish the nature of his own discourse (one that reveals the play of domination) from the discourses about which he writes (those that institute systems of domination). The demand for such a distinction raises subtle interpretive questions which cannot be adequately treated here, although some clarification of the issues can be attempted. Foucault, like Nietzsche, insists that reason is implicated in power. Therefore his own discourse is a form of power. Nothing prevents Foucault, who recognizes this state of affairs, from self-consciously reflecting on the power implication of his own discourse, of making explicit his political position and attempting to account for the conditions of its possibility.

The concept of discourse and the critique of reason are features of Foucault's texts that relate without difficulty to the present conjuncture. The third element in the task of situating these texts — the mode of information — involves a more remote and indirect association. In a very general way Foucault's texts pose the question of language in relation to society. They thread a thin line between the traditional Marxist emphasis on action (praxis, labor) and the Western Marxist problematic of ideology and the superstructure. Foucault's category discourse/practice draws the attention of critical theory to systems of language as they are related to and shape experience. Surveillance, the confessional, psychoanalysis — these are 'technologies of power' that have their great effect through their linguistic permutations. Surveillance, for example, is accomplished by setting in place a flow of information from the object under scrutiny to the authorities and to the collection of that information in files or memory banks. The existence of this network of information and the awareness of it by the scrutinized population constitutes the technology of power. Domination here takes the form, not of personal control (feudalism), nor of structural manipulation of activity (capitalism), but of complex articulation of language.

I employ the term mode of information to designate forms of linguistic experience that have emerged in the course of the twentieth century. The analysis of these linguistic forms and their relations with other social levels (work, family politics, leisure) must be placed high on the agenda of critical theory. As Raymond Williams has astutely observed. 'The major modern communication systems are now so evidently key institutions in advanced capitalist socieities that they require the same kind of attention, at least initially, that is given to the institutions of industrial production and distribution.'[15]

In the context of the analysis of the mode of information Foucault's recent texts assume their full importance. The mode of information provides the historical conditions of possibility for the category discourse/practice. At the same time the category discourse/practice provides the best interpretive framework for the analysis of the mode of information. This statement must remain at the hypothetical level, simply because the category discourse/practice has not been applied self-consciously to the mode of information. I am proposing it as a suggestion for future studies, and also as a contextual support for *Discipline and Punish* and *The History of Sexuality*. My position may be summed up as follows: Marxist and Western Marxists need to pay heed to these texts because they are the best examples of critical social theory in the age of the mode of information. Foucault's texts do not work to undermine capitalism; they are not adequate as class analysis; they do not provide a link between the superstructure and the substructure; they do not expose the ideological play behind the culture industry. Yet for all this they remain key works in the development of a critical theory of advanced society.

Face to face interactions with oral exchanges of symbols,

supplemented by written communications, have diminished in the texture of social life. In their place a variety of communication patterns have come into existence. These may be enumerated and analyzed according to their progressive dissimilarity to the older types. Telephone conversations are perhaps the most like pre-existing forms of communication. In this case verbal interchange occurs, but one through a gap of physical separation. However, one completely new form of interaction is made possible through the telephone: strangers may present themselves through their voices alone. A stranger obtains the opportunity for dialogue that in the past was reserved for acquaintances and those who were admitted to verbal interchange by the individual's decision to do so.

Still further removed from the traditional communication form is the television 'conversation'. Superficially a monologue, television communication contains many of the features of dialogue in that the viewer-listener is changed by the experience: he or she has consumed meanings. Television, of course, consists in visual and verbal messages which are received at the discretion of the viewer-listener. Here the visual image and voice of a stranger can enter one's home, simulating the visit of a friend. Once again the expansion of communicational forms relativizes the traditional forms: a friend's visit may contain less meaning, be less important than the visit of an electric emission. Social reality then changes its shape: social interactions are a combination of face-to-face verbal exchanges and electronic audio-visual emissions. Are both then equally real or important for the individual? How are the prospects of democratic community changed by the existence of the new melange of communication forms?

Perhaps furthest removed from the traditional language experience is the 'conversation' between two information processing machines or computers. In this case there is no physical presence and no verbal exchange. A simulation of written information, processed by complex permutations, is exchanged from one machine to another. Yet this information can be about human beings in society. The exchange between the machines must be counted as part of the linguistic experience of the society. In fact, it may, in a particular case, affect the lives of certain individuals very deeply, more than face-to-face conversations between friends. The machines, for example, may be gathering and exchanging information about the qualifications of an individual for welfare payments, or medi-care, or the record of a criminal, or the credit history of a businessman. In these cases the outcome of the machine's conversation may decisively influence the life of an individual. Machine conversations are part of our linguistic community: they constitute an increasing portion of our social interactions. As members of our linguistic world, what is their relation to a democratic community?

The language form unique to the mode of information that receives most attention today is that of individual to computer. In the past few years, millions have attained 'computer literacy', the ability to communicate in the 'foreign' language of the newest 'immigrants'. The computer presents fascinating questions for analysis. Its linguistic and epistemological status are by no means clear despite the flurry of essays, for and against, on the question of computer intelligence. An analogy with Marx's analysis of the machine is appropriate. The computer stores not dead labor but dead knowledge. It replaces not the arms and muscles of the worker but his or her mental functions of memory and calculation, among others. It stands against the living worker, to continue the Marxist analogy, like his or her alien essence, dominating the work process. The reversal of priorities Marx saw in the factory whereby the dead (machines) dominate' the living (workers) is extended by the computer to the realm of knowledge.

The linguistic relation of computer and individual goes beyond this comparison. Like mechanical machines, the computer shapes the mind of its user; unlike older contrivances, it engages the user's consciousness. Its powers seem to enchant users who become absorbed by the capabilities it offers. The line dividing subject and object is blurred, far more than it was in Marx's analysis of labor.[16] Which is the subject, computer or individual? Which has the capacity to generate knowledge, has greater mental powers? Whence comes the fascination users seem to derive from conversations with unknown partners through the mediation of computers?[17]

These are obviously a few of the new forms of language experiences that now inhabit our social landscape. They concern only the changed linguistic form itself, excluding any discussion of the interplay between the linguistic form and other social levels. For example, there is the relation of the new linguistic forms to the world of work,[18] the mode of production, as was discussed briefly in chapter 2. There is also the relation of the new linguistic forms to the world of leisure and consumption. One need only mention in this regard the proliferation of electronic game arcades and the spread of advertising through television. Finally, there is the relation of the new linguistic forms to the political world. In chapter 4 I discussed the importance of the new mode of surveillance, an extension of the Panopticon, made possible by computer conversations. In these respects the new linguistic forms have an increasingly larger impact on all the major institutions of advanced society.

Taken together, the study of the new forms of language experience and the relation of these new forms to other social institutions constitutes the substance of the term 'mode of information'. I am not arguing that the mode of information completely replaces the mode of production: society could not continue without the uninterrupted production of commodities. Nor am I arguing that the mode of information is the only or even central concern of critical theory. Questions of nuclear war and ecological balance with nature must remain the top priorities of critical inquiry for obvious reasons. What I am saying is rather that the social field is changing rapidly, that new forms of social interaction based on electronic communications devices are replacing older types of social relations and that the place of language experience is an important area in the new social fabric. Therefore critical theory must take cognizance of the novelty of the situation and reconstitute its conceptual orientation accordingly. Marxism, clutching to the theory of the mode of production, does not provide seminal pathways into the new social world.[19]

Foucault's discourse analysis takes on its full significance for critical theory when the mode of information is taken into account. The emergence and spread of the new linguistic experiences constitute the historical conditions for a method of analysis that gives due recognition to the discursive nature of practice, that conceptualizes truth in relation to power, that detotalizes the historical-social field and that sets strict limits to the scope of reason, reason both as analytic power and as the shape of consciousness in human beings acting in the social field. Foucault's interpretive strategy is particularly suited to a social field pervaded by linguistically rich forms of action. Alternative methods err in two opposite directions: (1) they analytically constitute language in formalist schemes that obscure the social context and the action component of experience, or (2) they give priority to action in a manner that obscures the linguistic quality of experience. Structuralist, semiotic and literary approaches generally move in the first direction; Marxist tendencies move in the second direction. Foucault's recent work steers a course between the dangers of idealist Scylla and materialist Charybdis. His position makes intelligible a level of analysis consonant with emergent forms of social relations. *Discipline and Punish* and *The History of Sexuality* have generated so much interest, I believe, because they speak so directly to the present conjuncture, providing a genuinely critical perspective on a social world that is resistant to intellectual formations like liberalism and Marxism that are rooted in assumptions of a bygone era. The mode of information renders obsolete positions which depict human beings as rational ghosts in corporal machines or laboring animals acting against nature in an alienating social fabric.

NOTES

1. See the delightful piece of Jacques Léonard, 'L'Historien et le philosophe', in *L'Impossible Prison*, ed. Michelle Perrot (Paris: Editions du Seuil, 1980), pp. 9–28, where a parody of the traditional historian's criticism of Foucault's work is presented and criticized.
2. See the interviews in *Power/Knowledge*.
3. This is the perspective of Pierre Bourdieu in *Outline of a Theory of Practice*, trans. Richard Nice (New York: Cambridge University Press, 1977) and Michel de Certeau in *L'Invention du quotidien: I. Arts de faire* (Paris: 10/18, 1980). A critique similar to mine is made by Nicos Poulantzas in *State, Power, Socialism*, trans. Patrick Camiller (London: New Left Books, 1978), p. 79.
4. *Discipline and Punish*, p. 23.
5. Easton and Guddat, eds., *The Writings of the Young Marx on Philosophy and Society*, (New York: Anchor, 1967), p. 431.
6. Theodor Adorno and Max Horkheimer, *Dialectic of Enlightenment*, trans. John Cumming (New York: Seabury, 1972, original edition 1944). Friedrich Nietzsche, *Beyond Good and Evil: Prelude to a Philosophy of the Future*, trans. Walter Kaufman (New York: Vintage, 1966).
7. See for example, Edward Said, 'Travelling Theory', *Raritan* (Winter, 1982), pp. 41–67.
8. For an attempt at a general theory of resistance, see Michel de Certeau, *L'invention du quotidien: I*.
9. M. Morris and Paul Patton (eds), *M. Foucault: Power, Truth, Strategy* (Sydney: Feral, 1979), p. 57 and Gwendolyn Wright and Paul Rabinow, 'Spatialization of Power: A Discussion of the Work of Michel Foucault', *Skyline* (March, 1982), pp. 14–20.
10. 'What is an Author?', in *Language, Counter-Memory, Practice* Don Bouchard (ed.) (Ithaca: Cornell University Press, 1977), pp. 113–38.

11. See the treatment of this problem by David Carroll in 'The Subject of Archeology or the Sovereignty of the Episteme', *Modern Language Notes*, No. 93 (1978), pp. 695–722.
12. *The Archeology of Knowledge*, p. 130.
13. Jean Baudrillard, *Oublier Foucault* (Paris: Editions Galilée, 1977), trans. *Humanities in Society*, 3 (Winter, 1980), pp. 87–111, notes this problem in Foucault's concept of power and uses it as the starting point of a general critique of Foucault's position, one that is not often convincing.
14. Foucault, 'History, Discourse, Discontinuity', *Salmagundi*, No. 20 (Summer – Fall, 1972), p. 241.
15. Raymond Williams, *Communications* (New York: Penguin, 1976) p. 136.
16. See Jean Zeitoun, 'Codes et langages pour un sujet terminal', in 'Les rhétoriques de la technologie', *Traverses*, 26 (October, 1982), pp. 72–9, for an interesting discussion of the exchange between individual and computer.
17. Andrew Feenberg, 'Moderating an Educational Teleconference', in M. Heimerdinger and M. Turoff (eds), *Educational Teleconferencing* (Norwood, New Jersey: Ablex, 1984).
18. See Gunter Friedrichs and Adam Schaff (eds), *Microelectronics and Society For Better or for Worse: A Report to the Club of Rome* (New York: Pergamon, 1982), especially Klaus Lenk, 'Information Technology and Society', pp. 273–310 and Ray Curnow and Susan Curran, 'The Technology Applied', pp. 89–118.
19. Barry Smart, *Foucault, Marxism and Critique* (London: Routledge and Kegan Paul, 1983) concludes with a similar judgement after an analysis that stresses the political dimension in comparing Marx with Foucault.

Index